GETTING GOOD AT BEING YOU

C. Sybil Waldrop

BROADMAN PRESS
Nashville, Tennessee

4250-40
ISBN: 0-8054-5040-8

Dewey Decimal Classification: 159
Subject Heading: PSYCHOLOGY, APPLIED
Library of Congress Catalog Card Number: 89-22381
Printed in the United States of America

Unless otherwise indicated all Scripture quotations are from the *New American Standard Bible.* ©The Lockman Foundation, 1960, 1962, 1963, 1968, 1971, 1972, 1973, 1975, 1977. Used by permission.

All Scripture quotations marked KJV are from the King James Version.

All verses marked TLB are taken from *The Living Bible.* Copyright © Tyndale House Publishers, Wheaton, Illinois, 1972. Used by permission.

All Scripture quotations marked GNB are from the *Good News Bible*, the Bible in Today's English Version. Old Testament: Copyright © American Bible Society 1976; New Testament: Copyright © American Bible Society 1966, 1971, 1976. Used by permission.

All Scripture quotations marked NIV are from the Holy Bible, *New International Version*, copyright © 1973, 1978, 1984 by International Bible Society.

Library of Congress Cataloging-in-Publication Data

Waldrop, C. Sybil.
    Getting good at being you/C. Sybil Waldrop.
       p. cm.
    ISBN 0-8054-5040-8
    1. Christian life—1960– 2. Love—Religious aspects—
Christianity. 3. Self-realization—Religious aspects—
Christianity. 4. Identification (Religion) I. Title.
BV4501.2.W288   1989
248.4—dc20
                                                    89–22381

To

my parents,
Annie Sanders Durbin and Benjamin Paul Durbin,
whose loving care assisted my
getting good* at being a child and a youth;
my husband, Fred,
whose supportive love enabled my getting good
at being a wife, educator, and
pastor's wife—all at the same time;
my children, Don, LeAnn, and Mark,
whose love, laughter, joys, and tears
aided my getting good at being a mother;
and all those who sought my counsel, whose trust
and openness encouraged my getting good
at being a counselor and friend.

*Getting good is a lifetime process of becoming all that God made you able to become. You are always striving toward becoming perfect—whole, complete, a more mature you.

Preface

Is this book for you? Take a moment and decide which of the following statements is true for you.

I am fascinated by the title of this book.

This is the book I have been waiting for.

I am ready for a change in my life.

Stop! If you chose any of the above statements, *this book is for you.*

Look! Which of the following questions have you asked?

What is life all about anyway?

Is there more to life than this?

What do I have to look forward to?

Do I ever do anything right?

Do I have talents?

Will I always be shy?

Which of the following feelings have you had?

I really would like to change, but I don't know how.

Nobody really cares about me.

If I don't expect anything of anybody, then I won't get hurt.

I am trapped and don't know what to do.

Nobody understands me.

Life is passing me by.

Life is a rat race.

I am on a merry-go-round; inside I am screaming, "Let me off!"

I am not happy with my life.

Something is missing in my life.

I need a change.

Listen! If you checked any of these statements, you may find one new or more new thoughts which challenges you, or an old idea which you have not yet tried. If, however, you have checked most or all, you may savor every moment you spend reading and responding to the thoughts conveyed through these pages.

Proceed with caution! You may never be the same again. "Happiness is a journey, not a destination." And as a book by the same title says, "Happiness is a choice." What better choice for happiness can you make than *getting good at being you!*

My thoughts, prayers, and blessing go with you as you go forth. I am traveling along with you out of my own inner struggle and quest for fulfillment, confidence, joy, and peace.

As I completed a series of messages on celebrating life, a young woman asked where she could buy the book containing my messages. There was no such book. Her inquiry prompted my need for writing it. I wrote it because I had to. This book was conceived in love, carried patiently over a period of months during the gestation period, and delivered with pain. I share the feeling of Robert Louis Stevenson who said, "I hate to write, but I love to have written." To me, happiness is to *have* written. This is the kind of book I needed to read many years ago. With the help of the One who enables me far beyond my imaginations, I have delivered this gift to you.

May God exceedingly bless you as you submit to His plan for your life and commit yourself to *getting good at being you.*

Full speed ahead! This book is designed for you to participate as you read. Let's take turns. I will talk to you for a while, that will be my turn. You will have the opportunity to respond—agree, disagree, interact, react, or simply share your own thoughts. That will be your turn. This is the time for you to reflect on and apply what you have read, understood, felt, or desired. Your answers are not necessarily right or wrong. Hopefully, they are *your* honest responses.

You may be tempted to read without responding in writing. The full benefit will be gained as you involve yourself. I trust that you will do what best fits your needs

Bon voyage!

CONTENTS

1

LOVE YOUR CREATOR

"It is He who has made us, and not we ourselves" (Ps. 100:3).

Who am I? Where did I come from? Who made me? Why am I here? Discovering the answers to these questions can be life changing. Join me in the exciting adventure of discovery. Ask yourself: Who am I *now*? Why am I here *now*? Life is dynamic, not static. The person you were yesterday, you no longer are. Your purpose for being alive today will be somewhat different from what it was yesterday. The specifics will change, the people with whom you relate may be different, and the circumstances will be unique to the moment.

You had no choice in being born. Neither did you choose your parents, nor did your parents choose their parents. Parents are instruments through whom life flows. The genes transferred from your parents to you were given to them. They came through someone else. All genes can be traced to a source—God. "In the beginning God" (Gen. 1:1).

CELEBRATE LIFE—YOURS

God Made You
YOUR TURN: Close your eyes, and for one minute think of words to describe God. Open your eyes and jot down the words. Now look at the words you wrote and answer these questions:

1. How many positive words did you write (words that reflect a loving God)? Cherish the truth: "God is love" (1 John 4:8). Jesus began what we call the Lord's Prayer with "Our Father." *Father* is a loving, affectionate, family word. Moses described God in this way: "His work is perfect, For all His ways are just; A God of faithfulness and without injustice, Righteous and upright is He" (Deut. 32:4).

2. How many negative words did you write (words that convey a punitive God—looking over your shoulder, ready to slap your hands at every mistake)? God is out to get you, but not in a punitive way. He wants to woo you to Himself. He wants the best for you. What you think about God largely determines (1) how you respond to Him, (2) what you think about yourself, and (3) what you think about others. How important it is that you know who God is and what God is like!

In His Image

You can celebrate your life because God made you, and He made you in His likeness. Mind-boggling! To think that you (and I) are made in God's image. Read it for yourself in Genesis 1:26-28a. Notice that *make* (v. 26) and *created* (v. 27) are used interchangeably in these verses.

3. In what ways are you like God (made in His likeness)? Pause and answer the question for yourself before you read further. God is all-powerful, all-wise, all-knowing, everywhere and at-all-times present, and most importantly, all-loving. Humans are not. How then are you made like Him? You are an autographed original. You bear His divine imprint. No one but the Almighty God could have made you so incredibly wonderful and unique.

God is orderly and predictable. You are experiencing the same cycle of human development common to all His human creations, yet you are unique—one-of-a-kind. You are body, mind, and spirit, but you are one person. You have a fleshly mortal body; an intelligent, rational mind; and your body houses an immortal personality, spirit, or soul which is distinctly yours. God became flesh (body) and dwelled among us. He was embodied in Jesus Christ. He conformed to the same developmental design which He created. There is no greater love.

You were made to have fellowship with God. Your spirit longs for His Spirit. The human spirit, unlike that of lower animals, seeks to know, love, worship, praise, thank, and adore its Maker.

God remains the same yesterday, today, and forever. He is dependable. His creation is dynamic (ever changing) and perpetual (continuing forever). You are always changing. How fascinating life is! Each moment provides you with numerous opportunities for maturing and developing new insights and skills with which to face life with joy and expectancy. The gift of life is indeed a cause to celebrate. Flood your thoughts with this grand truth: God made me. God made me what I can be. Children sing these words, often with gusto. Try singing or saying them with gusto. What you say (or sing) to yourself, you tend to believe; what you believe, you act upon. You can choose to believe and act as if you were created by the Maker of heaven and earth and made in His likeness. Because you were.

In a notebook or on a piece of paper write a sentence which best describes your feelings toward the Divine Creator who gave you the gift of life.

CELEBRATE YOUR INHERITANCE

Your inheritance from your earthly parents may be one of poverty or wealth. You are not created equal to others by virtue of your material possessions. Your inheritance from God, however, is a life in His wonderful world—a vast, infinite universe— which is shared with all humans. Can anyone else enjoy its riches more than you? If so, why? God made the world for you to enjoy, to explore, to discover, to use, and to preserve. He put you in a laboratory supplied with endless resources and has challenged you to conquer and subdue. Each generation succeeds in new discoveries. Each new discovery becomes the threshold for another. The impossible becomes the possible.

My astronomy professor in the late forties gave us detailed reasons why going to the moon was impossible—too many calculations to coordinate and lack of a suitable fuel which could be stored in the necessary quantity. We were told that the earth turns on its axis, making a complete revolution in twenty-four hours. The moon which also turns revolves around the earth. The earth and its moon move in orbit around the sun, the center of the solar system. The solar system, a part of the Milky Way, also moves forth in space. How do you calculate the speed of an object moving inside earth's gravity pull and outside the pull of gravity with all the movement occurring?

A few decades later, however, men walked on the moon. Commander Neil Armstrong, of *Apollo 11*, said as he stepped onto the

moon, "That's one small step for a man, one giant leap for mankind."
Today space stations patterned after earth's environment are being
prepared to house a space community for a period of years. Awesome
is the possibility that what is fiction today becomes reality tomorrow.
God has given us immense intelligence, which when used cooperatively over time, results in feats beyond our human understanding. How
marvelous are Your works, O God!

Getting good at being you means getting acquainted with your
Maker and His matchless creation. How refreshing, liberating, and
humbling to sense the awe and wonder of the natural world, unspoiled
by the work of human hands.

Sometimes I pause from my labor to recharge my energies. Seeking
stillness and quietness, I find my way to our small patio equipped with
only one recliner. Here I sit or lie to survey the magnificent beauty of
the changing clouds both overhead and beyond the tree-covered hills.
My eyes are attracted to the movement of the green leaves swaying
listlessly. My body feels the coolness of a breeze which I cannot see.
With a blue sky above and green trees around me, I bask in the relaxing pleasantness of His matchless design. I sit entranced and exhilarat-
ed by the majestic splendor which invades my senses.

Through His creation, God communicates

His wisdom,

His love,

His righteousness (His right actions on our behalf),

His mercy (He has adequately supplied us with resources and the
        intelligence with which to use them),

His patience and long-suffering, and

His sense of humor.

When you seek God and desire to become aware of what He is saying through creation, you are in the process of growing, developing,
and becoming what He made you uniquely able to become.

Listen to the question posed by the psalmist at the end of his statement: "When I consider Thy heavens [stretching to infinity], the work
of Thy fingers, the moon [on which human feet recently walked] and
the stars [billions of billions in number, ranging in distance from tril-
lions of miles to millions of light years, grouped by billions in galaxies

which number millions of millions], which Thou hast ordained; *What is man [living on the infinitesimally small planet earth], that Thou dost take thought of him?"* (Ps. 8:3-4, author's italics).

Hear the psalmist answer his own question about the importance of man: "Yet Thou hast made him a little lower than God, And dost crown him with glory and majesty! Thou dost make him to rule over the works of Thy hands; Thou hast put all things under his feet" (Ps. 8:5-6).

Wow! How humbling. Thus God communicates: "You are very special to Me. I made you. I made you in My image. I love you. I have given you a magnificent world. This is My inheritance to you. Use, enjoy, discover, learn, become the person I made you to be. Deliver the message for which I sent you into the world. Love Me, and keep My Commandments (They are for your good.). I am in control. I watch over you. I care for you. You can depend on Me. You can trust that I want the best for you. Keep on becoming, living fully, and sharing My love."

Receive your inheritance. It is God's gift to His children. Savor the expressions of His love and compassion.

Just yesterday I took a walk away from the workplace, from the busy tedium of handling seemingly endless tasks and from the constant stream of people entering my door. My need for privacy and solitude found me on a downtown street crowded with noonday shoppers. On the sidewalk, I found my retreat and paused momentarily to sit alone on a bench beside a small graceful tree. My eyes turned toward the movement of a bird which landed near my feet. The tiny bird began feeding on the seed which had fallen from the tree. How could this tiny bird in flight see the tiny seed camouflaged against the gray cobblestones? For a brief and enthralling time, God spoke loudly to me in His silence. *God, how great You are to turn my thoughts toward You at the sight of a petite brown bird.* I saw in that small creature the creative work of the Master of the universe and recalled the words of Jesus: "Look at the birds of the air, that they do not sow, neither do they reap, nor gather into barns, and yet your heavenly Father feeds them. Are you not worth much more than they?" (Matt. 6:26).

The person who is growing toward maturity (becoming perfect—

complete, whole, more Godlike) is intrigued with God's handiwork
and finds solace and strength from meditating on God's greatness and
goodness. As you behold the wonders of creation, your heart will
surge with praise, worship, thankfulness, peace, and joy.

As a young child, the most delightful and memorable experience I
had with God's handiwork was watching tadpoles change into frogs.
When I was growing up, my father was pastor of four and five churches at a time. When he preached away from our hometown, we would
spend the afternoon with a family who attended the local church. One
of my favorite things to do was to find a glass jar and walk along the
road in search of a puddle of water where I could find frog eggs—little
black balls—each protected by a coat of transparent jelly. Carefully, I
would place the jar mouth beneath my wonderful discovery and gather the eggs undisturbed into the jar. Day by day I would watch as tiny
black balls changed into wiggling tadpoles which grew bigger and bigger. A long tail developed and gradually disappeared as legs formed.
Soon tiny amphibious frogs emerged. Such a dramatic transformation!
Later I learned the term *metamorphosis* to describe this change.

I now know that God can work in you (and me) this same dramatic
transformation. God made you to become fully you. Consider the
change that has occurred in you from birth. The outward transformations are striking. The inward transformations are and can be equally
striking or more so. You can become fully alive by fully discovering
who you are, who you were meant to be, and the gifts which God has
given you. If God can change a tadpole into a frog, just think what He
can do with you, the highest of His creation.

YOUR TURN: Think about your favorite childhood experience with
nature. Record you feelings and impressions in your notebook or on a
sheet of paper. What can/did you learn about God from this experience? During a recent conference, I invited participants to heighten
their awareness of God by taking a walk outside and talking to a tree.
Some responded with giggles at such a suggestion. One woman took
me seriously and returned with a powerful essay acclaiming God's
majesty, power, and love.

Have you ever wondered why God designed a flower whose blos-
soms, so long in coming, last only for a day, a week, or a short season?

Just think of the message a flower delivers. One floral company knows the message a flower gives and uses the slogan: "Say it with flowers." God has been saying it with flowers since the beginning. Each flower is a divine masterpiece of art. God's art gallery is always open for those who choose to look and see. The displays are constantly changing. The Artist remains the same. He declares in colorful, intricate design and texture His continual affection to us.

YOUR TURN: Think about and write down an answer to the question posed by the book title *What Do You Say When You Meet a Flower?* Several years ago a Sunday School teacher of small children experienced the untimely death of her husband. In a moment of desperate grief, feeling somehow that God had forsaken her, she looked out a window just in time to see a squirrel scampering up a tree. The words of a song which she had sung many times to children came rushing into her mind. The song went something like this: "If God so loves the little squirrels and shows them what to do, I know He loves me too." Suddenly her despair was replaced with comfort, hope, and the bliss of love.

My conscious remembrance of reverence for the things God made began during my college years when I read about Albert Schweitzer's "reverence for life." He impressed upon me that each living creature is a part of God's all-wise plan and is thus worthy of respect. When I discover an ant in the house, I gently remove it to the outside. When I share this idea in conferences, people seem surprised. "You've got to be kidding!" Testing the reality of my "reverence for life," their first question usually is, "But what do you do when you see a cockroach?" I counter their question with a question: "What do you think?"

As you become more and more aware of the beauty, design, and wisdom in the things God has made, you will become more willing to accept what He wants to make of you. To study His creation is to learn more about Him. The more you know of Him and His love, the more you want to know.

More about God's love will be discussed in the next chapter, "Love Yourself." To discuss the subject of loving yourself apart from the subject of loving God (the Source who gave you life) would be futile.

YOUR TURN: What have you read thus far that assures you of God's love for you? Make note of what you remember and look back through the chapter to see other ideas.

"We love, because He first loved us" (1 John 4:19). His great love surrounds us. The greatest love affair you can have is with your Creator. Unlike earthly love, this love will never disappoint you. It surpasses time. Your choice is to love or not to love. If you choose to love God, your next choice is: "How will you love God?" The first and great commandment sheds light on how you are to love God. "You shall love the Lord your God with all your heart and with all your soul and with all your might" (Deut. 6:5). When Jesus quoted this commandment, He used two more words: *mind* (Matt. 22:37) and *strength* (Mark 12:30).

YOUR TURN: In what ways can you love God with your heart? your soul? your might (strength)? your mind? Getting good at being you begins with a love for your Heavenly Father who is your Creator and Redeemer. God loved us so much that when He had prepared the world, He conformed Himself to the same design of human development which we experience. Born of a woman, He grew through all the stages of life: childhood, youth, adult. His life is our example. He practiced what He preached about love. He allowed Himself to be tempted in all the ways we are tempted, yet He did not sin. He lived, loved, died, arose from the dead, and ascended into heaven. Jesus (God incarnate—in the flesh) said, "For God so loved the world, that He gave His only begotten Son, that whoever believes in Him should not perish, but have eternal life. For God did not send the Son into the world to judge the world; but that the world should be saved through Him" (John 3:16-17). God chose to come to earth to be one of us. He was born in a lowly stable. His crib was an animal's feed trough. His birth was announced to lowly men, the shepherds. He was born in a small village which was not the seat of culture, politics, nor religion. Mary and Joseph offered two doves (the sacrifice permitted of the poor) when Jesus was presented in the Temple as a child. Surely the poorest among us can identify with Him. He loved all people, including His enemies. He had a servant's attitude and ministry. He even washed His disciples' feet. What is more humbling? Peter summed up Jesus' ministry by saying, "He went about doing good" (Acts 10:38).

Dear God, thank You for making me.

Thank You for letting me live in the world in just such a time as this.

I do want to love You with all my heart (my feelings, emotions, motivations), my soul (my immortal spirit and personality), my mind (my intellect), and my strength (the energy and power of body, mind, and spirit)—with my total being. I want to joyfully proceed on my journey of getting good at being me. I want to experience enlightenment, fulfillment, joy, peace, love without partiality, and ultimate happiness. I am not finished yet. You are not finished with me yet. I am always in the process of becoming. Continue making me all I am able to become. I await each moment expectantly knowing that You will work in me and through me. You and I together are enough for any situation. I rest my case. I confidently rely on Your power within me. Thank You for Your great love to me. Again, I love You, God.

If you can make this prayer yours, then copy it in your notebook and sign your name to it.

2

LOVE YOURSELF

"For the whole Law is fulfilled in one word, in the statement, 'You shall love your neighbor as yourself' " (Gal. 5:14).

A few years ago I was invited to speak to an interdenominational Sunday School meeting on the subject: "Be All You Can Be." I began the session by inviting the people to sing with me this simple song: "I like me. I like me. I like the way that God made me. I like me." I asked the participants to think of three things they liked about themselves. They were asked to work in pairs. Each would share for thirty seconds three things he liked about himself and listen to the other share for thirty seconds. Some giggled nervously at what was perhaps their first experience at thinking about what they liked about themselves.

Following the speech a tall, strong-looking man in his early thirties dressed in western attire down to his cowboy boots approached me with teary eyes. Giving me a hug of gratitude, he revealed: "You are the only person who ever told me that I was valuable and worthwhile. I shall always remember."

This was not the first nor the last person who has shared such a comment. While leading a recent conference on the importance of self-esteem in the early years of life, a shy teacher of preschoolers in her fifties, uttered in a sad and broken voice, "How I wish someone had taught me as a child that I was valuable and worthwhile!" Regretful that she could have been a more radiant and caring person, she felt that she had wasted most of an important life. I believe the world is full of unhappy, anxious, miserable people who do not know they are valuable and worthwhile, and that it's OK to love themselves.

YOUR TURN: Pause long enough to write three things you like about yourself.

18

"YOU SHALL LOVE YOUR NEIGHBOR AS YOURSELF" (MATT. 22:39).

If you apply the second great commandment, you will love yourself. As you show love to yourself, you will find how wonderful it feels to be loved. You will feel an urgent need to share this love with another.

REAL JOY?

A rather familiar expression spoken from the pulpit declares, "Real JOY means loving Jesus first, others second, and yourself last." When I hear this I have an uneasy feeling. These questions come to my mind: Does *love* which brings real joy really happen in a one, two, three sequence? Can you love God and not love yourself? Do you do the three of these at the same time? Can you love your neighbor before you first love yourself? My heart's desire for you is that you can know *real* joy. Let us discover together the source of this joy.

While teaching the preschool Sunday School teachers in a church, I was also invited to dialogue with the kindergarten teachers who had just returned from their first national professional meeting. I inquired, "Well, what was the most exciting thing you heard during the entire meeting?"

One teacher was quick to respond. "Our conference leader said that it is all right to love yourself. And if no one else shows love to you, just stand in front of the mirror in the morning and give yourself a great big hug and say, 'I love you, (calling yourself by name).' "

I thought but did not say aloud, *What an indictment on the status of our love needs!* Who would have thought that these people did not feel loved enough? Feeling loved is our most basic human need. God planned that an irresistible baby born to loving parents would receive the necessary love during the earliest years. A child who experiences love during the first years of life is best able to enjoy life and to cope with later difficulties in life. If a child is not loved during the first years of life, receiving love and feeling loved becomes increasingly more difficult. If a child does not receive adequate love during the earliest days, months, and years of life, that child will behave in ways to meet that need. The behaviors may be annoying, destructive, and self-defeating. Those who feel loved by their earthly parents find it easier to accept the love of their Heavenly Father. Unless your need for love is met, you are a deprived person. There is no greater deprivation than that of love. Even a child born prematurely will not live, cannot thrive, without the warm, gentle, loving strokes of another human being.

You do not have to attend a national professional meeting to learn how to love yourself. You can start right now.

YOU CAN LOVE YOURSELF BECAUSE . . .

God Made You and Loves You

You are a child of God by means of creation. God loves you, and surely you want to love one whom God loves. God is love; and God offers His love unconditionally, with no strings attached. Choose to accept God's love. He wants you to experience real joy in this world and real hope for the world to come. When you accept His love, you can truly love yourself.

God Made You in His Likeness

You can feel valuable and worthwhile because God made you in His likeness. We call this feeling of worth and value *self-esteem* or high personal regard. Self-esteem is basic to mental health, to self-discipline, and to a productive life.

YOUR TURN: Pause now and assess your own self-esteem. Consider each rectangle a room in the house. Which room do you live in most of the time? Remember, each room has doors, and you may move from one to another. You can choose your favorite room. Think of an example in real life which illustrates the behavior of a person in each of the four rooms.

Read the description for each room in the columns on pages 21-22. Look at "The Self-Esteem House" on page 21. Decide which column describes each room.

THE SELF-ESTEEM HOUSE

What room do you live in?

I am valuable and worthwhile.

Room 4 low self-esteem masked by superiority *I am important.* *You are not important.*	Room 1 high self-esteem *I am important.* *You are important.*
Room 3 low self-esteem *You are not important.* *I am not important.*	Room 2 low self-esteem *You are important.* *I am not important.*

I am not valuable and worthwhile.

A. parenting style—overly
     permissive
  indulgent
  slave
  helpless
  indecisive
  does not value uniqueness
  patterns after others
  little or not self-respect
  afraid
  insecure
  "Help me."
  "Tell me what to do"
  little "I,"*low self-esteem*
  little "I," big "you"

C. parenting style—authorative
     approach (protector and
     guide)
  gets on with life
  friendly
  winner
  can see from viewpoint of
     another
  feels safe and secure
  lets others be themselves
  no need to control
  caring
  a feeling of *us*ness (we are in
     this together
  can be a leader or a follower

as needed

democratic

servant attitude

B. parenting style—   D. parenting style—inconsistent
     authoritarian   chip on the shoulder
   controlling (uses power over   abusive
     others)   hostile
   domineering—do as I say   hopeless
   big "I," little "you"   negligent
   egotistical   gets nowhere
   self-centered (has difficulty   little respect for self or
     seeing from view point of   others
     another)   hurts others

answers: A.2; B.4; C.1; D.3.

YOUR TURN: Read the following questions, answering yes or no to each one. If your answer is yes, decide which room you live in.

1. Are you overly concerned about what others think of you?
2. Are you primarily interested in others for what they can do for you?
3. Would you hurt someone and risk hurting yourself to get even?
4. Are you always telling others what to do, taking charge?
5. Do you accept another person's feelings and opinions?
6. Are you willing to do unto others as you would have others do unto you?

Possible answers: 1.2; 2.4,3,2; 3.3; 4.4; 5.1;6.1.

SELF-LOVE: WHAT IS IT?

I find myself disagreeing with those who proclaim: "What's wrong with the world is: 'We love ourselves too much. The world is full of too much self-love.' " I listen and talk to myself; and I say, "No, what is wrong with the world is there is not enough self-love. People do not love themselves enough." I think that we must mean different things when we use the words *self-love*. Perhaps they are trying to communicate that the world is too full of selfish people. Self-serving, selfish adults do not love themselves. They are falsely labeled. Maybe those who condemn self-love are referring to an obsession with one's self which is described in Greek mythology? The young Narcissus was punished by being forced to "fall in love" with his own reflection in the water. This kind of love(?)—stuck on oneself—is indeed punishment. A person impressed with his or her physical beauty has a false perception of what is really important. This person lacks love and real joy.

WHAT LOVING YOURSELF DOES NOT MEAN

Loving yourself does not mean indulgence. Indulgence is a characteristic of self-hate. Indulgence is an abuse to the body, mind, and spirit. When you hurt one part of you, you hurt all parts. You indulge yourself when you give in excessively to sensual desires and overeat,"overpleasurize,"oversleep or other words you may want to add. If you love yourself, you respect your body as the "temple of God" (see 1 Cor. 3:17). You want to care for it.

Loving yourself does not mean exploitation. Exploitation is overexerting, overusing, or over-extending the body at unnecessary times. It also means using the body in other ways that are unhealthy and harmful. For example, denying what the body needs in order to look skinny (equated with attractiveness) is an unhealthy goal.

Also, when you love yourself, you do not feel the need to exploit other persons. Parents sometimes use their children to meet their own needs. Those who pressure their children in the academics, in sports, or in the performing arts in order to boost their own egos are exploiting or using their children. When you love yourself you do not need to use your children as if they were trophies of your worth and value. You are happy and rejoice with them over their accomplishments, but you do not have to broadcast their achievements. You are happy to answer when others ask about your children. You do not need to live through your children. You do not need your children to make good grades to make you look good. Mainly, you want them to *learn* so that they can be happy, productive people.

When you love yourself, you can love your spouse, your child, and your best friend because they are persons of value and worth—not because of their performances. Paradoxically, when you do this, you free them to be themselves and to perform more ably.

WHEN YOU LOVE YOURSELF . . .

1. You know your value and worth. You know who you are and why you are here.

2. You respect yourself as one made in God's image (likeness).

3. You are aware of your gifts and cultivate them.

4. You do not have to compete or compare yourself with anyone. "But let each one examine his own work, and then he will have reason for boasting in regard to himself alone, and not in regard to another" (Gal. 6:4).

5. You discipline yourself. Basic to self-discipline is a knowledge of the truth that life is not easy. A disciplined person learns (1) to be self-controlled (accountable); (2) to delay pleasure when work should come first; (3) to balance work with recreation or variety; and (4) to develop mind, body, and spirit knowing that growing toward maturity is a continual challenge.

6. You expect the best. Your motto is that of William Carey who said, "Expect great things from God. Attempt great things for God." When you expect good things to happen, they do. When you expect bad things to happen, they do. So begin now to expect the best in people and in the experiences of the day. Do this knowing that God will work good from all the experiences of our life, even though the experiences may not seem good at the time (see Rom. 8:28).

7. You are free to forget yourself. You are not self-conscious or self-absorbed. You are in the best position to forget yourself, see the needs of others, and to give yourself to meeting those needs.

8. You accept responsibility for your actions, even accepting blame when you are at fault.

9. Your conversations are positive, uplifting, and enhancing.

10. You do not criticize. You know that all people are human, and all people make mistakes. And that includes you, too.

11. You know that others are valuable and worthwhile. You are not better than anyone else, but you are different from everyone else.

12. Your mission is to help others know that they are valuable and worthwhile and that they, too, are worthy of love.

13. You need praise less and less. You do not need to sound a trumpet before you so that others notice your "good works." What you do for others is solely to meet a need. A woman recuperating from surgery called me to see if I had sent her the yellow roses which were delivered without a card. She wanted to thank the person who sent them. I said: "Obviously, this person did not want you to know. The person just wanted to cheer you."

14. You are humble. You do not think more highly of yourself than you ought to think. "For if anyone thinks he is something when he is nothing, he deceives himself" (Gal. 6:3).

15. Love is wanting the best for every person, and that includes you.

YOUR TURN: The following list is from 1 Corinthians 13. Read each characteristic of love and rate yourself from 1 to 5 (*one* being the least, and *five* being the most). Ask yourself, "How have I shown in my actions or in my attitudes today that I possess these traits?" Write each characteristic in your notebook or on a sheet of paper and write your answer beside the appropriate characteristic.

Love . . .
    is patient
    is kind
    is not jealous
    does not brag
    is not arrogant
    does not act unbecomingly
    is not easily provoked
    does not take into account a wrong suffered
    does not rejoice in unrighteousness
    rejoices in truth
    bears all things
    believes all things
    hopes all things
    endures all things
    never fails

YOUR TURN: Read the following statements. Which ones can you use to help you love yourself?

1. I can remember who made me. God did. The great Creator Diety. What a humbling, yet ecstatic, thought.

2. I can tell myself how wonderfully and fearfully God made me.

3. I can tell myself that I am a Designer's original—unique, different from anyone else in the world.

4. I can remember that God has a plan for me. I will assess my gifts and determine what I can doto exercise and use my gifts.

5. I will discover God's plan for me. (The plan may include different kinds of work: the work I do for a livelihood, the work I do in my family, church, community, or world. The plan may change throughout my life.)

6. I can notice God's gifts in nature and feel and hear God's message of love to me.

7. I can show respect (high regard) for myself as God's creation—a temple in whom God dwells.

Add other statements as you begin to show love to yourself. Also, write what you will do specifically about each. Your list may begin something like this:

• be open to experience—an avid learner (I will keep a list of what I want to know or learn.)
• not overextend myself
• involve myself wholeheartedly in life
• show interest in others
• eat wisely (right foods, appropriate times, appropriate quantity)
• get enough sleep and rest
• use my time wisely
• pace activities
• spend time in recreation to reenergize and renew myself

Each of us needs something to look forward to. We may need an escape from difficult work, some spice in life, or a time for necessary reflection. Escape may bring relief from pressures, reflection may help you deal with them. If you want to show love to yourself, take excellent care of your body, mind, and spirit. God has given you this blessed stewardship.

Real joy is accepting God's love, loving God with all your being, loving yourself as fearfully and wonderfully made with a special mission to accomplish, and loving others with a self-giving (not self-serving) motive. Amazingly, as you lose your life, you find life more exceedingly abundant than ever before. You feel so fortunate to be radiantly alive. You enjoy being who you are. You would not exchange places with anyone else anywhere.

3

LOVE OTHERS

"You shall love your neighbor as yourself" (Mark 12:31).

"I like you.
I like you.
God made me and
God made you.
I like you."

When my husband was pastoring his home church, we were expecting our second child. Being threatened with a miscarriage, I was ordered to bed by my doctor. Wanting to help in any way she could, Clifford Alford, a member of the church came to our house to take care of me. Knowing that I needed a bath, she did not hesitate to give me one. How refreshing was the warm water and the soft texture of the cloth on my body! When she began bathing my feet, a deeper humility than I had ever before felt invaded my soul. More refreshing to my spirit than water to my body was her gentle, loving care. In my helplessness, she came to me. Nothing was too menial or lowly for her to do. Her act of humility and love reminded me of the time when Jesus washed His disciples' feet. When Peter questioned Jesus, "Lord, do You wash my feet?" Jesus responded, "If I then, the Lord and the Teacher, washed your feet, you also ought to wash one another's feet" (John 13:6,13).

LOVE AND ETERNAL LIFE

When a teacher of the law asked Jesus what he must do to have eternal life, Jesus answered with these questions: "What is written in the Law? How does it read to you?" (Luke 10:26).

The lawyer cited the Law: "You shall love the Lord your God with all your heart, and with all your soul, and with all your strength, and with all your mind: and your neighbor as yourself" (Luke 10:27).

Jesus responded, "You have answered correctly; do this, and you will live" (Luke 10:28).

When the lawyer tried to justify himself by asking "Who is my neighbor?" Jesus told him about a man who was left half dead by some robbers. Men of three different professions saw the man lying on the road.

YOUR TURN: Read Luke 10:30-37 and answer the questions: Who was the man in verse 31? How would you have expected him to help? What did the man do? Read verse 32 and answer the same three questions. Read verse 33 and answer the questions again.

The third man was from an area called Samaria. The Samaritans were part Jewish. Jews despised Samaritans. They did not accept Samaritans as Jews. Today similar prejudices exist.)

Notice that when Jesus finished the story, He did not answer the lawyer's question. Rather Jesus focused attention on how to be a good neighbor by asking, "Which of these three do you think proved to be a neighbor?" (Luke 10:36). The lawyer learned both how he could be a good neighbor and who his neighbor was.

How can you be a good neighbor?

Who is your neighbor (the one you are to love)?

LOVE EXPECTS NO RETURN

What did the Samaritan expect to gain from his neighborliness? He did not know the man. He did not know his social status, religious belief, nor financial means. The Samaritan spent his time, effort, and resources, and he asked nothing in return. The test of love is your motive (your reason) for showing mercy and compassion. The first and second greatest commandments are inseparable. You cannot do one without the other. You cannot love God and not love the highest of His creation—yourself and others. You cannot love yourself and others without loving the Source from which you come. God is the Source of love. We are to love others because God made us all. He made us all in His image (likeness). Each human being is a Designer's original and bears the divine imprint or autograph.

Sing or say the words found at the beginning of the chapter. Can you make these words your words?

You may experience several kinds of love. As you read about each kind, think about examples from your own life to illustrate them. When you love someone because *you need them,* you love out of dependency. When you love someone because *you want them,* your love is to meet your desires. At this level, the physical attraction of another or your emotional needs prompts you to love. This self-needed, self-desired love is at the lowest level.

At a higher level of love, you may be attracted to another not primarily for physical or emotional desires but because you have kindred spirits and common interests. You enjoy being in the presence of the other. You may want the other's attention and love. You give love and expect something in return even though you may not be consciously aware of it. You may expect the other person to love you, or you may expect a good relationship or some other reward. This is a self-giving love with an expectation of receiving love or something in return.

At the highest level is *a Godlike love.* You love someone no matter what, with no strings attached. You love not because of what you can get, yet you always receive a blessing which far exceeds what you gave. You give because you want to meet the needs of another. This is self-giving love.

Lottie Moon, a missionary to China many years ago, would not keep enough food for herself when those around her were hungry. Her great love was costly. She died of starvation. Her joy was complete, and today her influence is still felt. Loving God with her whole being, she was free to deny herself and give herself away.

The level of love which you attain is in proportion to your love of God and self. The greater your love of God and self, the greater your freedom to forget yourself and give yourself to others. Indeed only when you lose your life do you really find it in all its fullness.

Learning to love is a developmental process. Love is not static. Love is dynamic—always changing. A person's level of thinking affects his ability to love. You may be at the highest level of thinking ability, however, and not love at the highest level. You may be a youth or an adult still behaving at a lower level. As you read the developmental stages of love, ask yourself: Where am I on the developmental scale of love?

Early Childhood (birth through age seven)

The literal child thinks mostly of the surface meaning of words. He notices how things look,taste, feel, smell, and sound. He learns about real things he experiences through the senses. For the child, kindness or love must be expressed in tangible ways. Love then is an action a hug, a kiss, a gentle touch or stroke, a smile, someone taking a turn with a toy or giving him a lick of ice cream. The child learns how to love from the important people in his early life. The mother kisses her infant on the cheek, and soon the child gives wonderful wet kisses on Mother's face. Mother responds with glee. She is ecstatic. She talks softly to the baby and cuddles her closer. The child continues to do that which gives her so much warm and affectionate attention from her mother. Such reward!

Young children are self-centered. This is not the same as selfish. The child sees only from his view. He cannot mentally get inside another person and think what that person is thinking. Much of children's annoying behavior is a result of their self-centered view. Two-year-old Tony has been told that his uncle who is home for Christmas will teach him how to ride the tricycle. Before Christmas dinner is over, Tony slips out of his chair and goes to his uncle. Tugging on Uncle's pant leg, Tony says, "Will you teach me to ride my tricycle now?" He does not know how important eating is to his uncle. He only knows that learning to ride his tricycle is important to him.

A child who stands between you and the television does not know he is blocking your view. He only sees what he sees. You will need to patiently say to him what is happening and suggest another place for him to stand.

Preschoolers do not think like adults think. When you put adult intent into a child's behavior, you may mistake it for moral badness when the child is behaving the best he knows how from his limited viewpoint. Parents are to be models of the behavior which they wish to teach. The burden of the learning is on the parent.

Self-centered preschoolers find it difficult to share. This is because they cannot see from the viewpoint of another. When you force a child to give up something to another, you are not teaching sharing. You are teaching force. Your child is learning, "When I get big, I can force other people to give up things to another." Isn't that what Robin Hood did? He took from the rich and gave to the poor. A child learns sharing by seeing parents share. If you want to teach sharing, help your children experience the joy of making something for another. Invite a child to help as you make bread or cookies for a neighbor. The child enjoys "cooking." She can enjoy eating some of what she "cooks," and then she can willingly give a portion to another. Love is best taught in the early years.

Childhood

What young children see, they believe. They do not take motives into account. If someone knocks over a block tower, the child notices what he sees happen. He does not know the difference between what is intentional or accidental.

During the years from about seven to twelve, the child becomes less self-centered as he has many experiences playing and working with others. He learns how others feel as his level of thinking increases. He is in a stage of "I'll take a turn, and you can take a turn" or "I'll give you a lick of my ice cream if you will let me taste yours."

A child at this age living with parents who model loving, sharing behavior may give and expect no tangible return. Seven-year-old Nathan was visiting his grandmother in a neighboring state. He heard someone say that last night a little statue of a boy fishing had been stolen from the neighbor's yard across the street. The previous day the child had become intrigued with the statue and had asked his grandmother to go with him to look at it. Now he was sad and wanted to help the man and woman feel better. Without telling anyone what he was doing, he painted a watercolor picture of the statue and asked his grandmother to take it to the neighbors. She agreed to walk with Nathan across the street, so he could share his gift of love and comfort. The child's reward was his feeling that he had done something to help a man and a woman at the time of their loss.

At this age children tend to believe in the idea of retribution—"an eye for an eye" or getting even. A motive of getting even is contrary to the motive of love which calls for loving your enemies—those who would hurt and use you. As a public school teacher, I would often hear a child say, "He hit me first." Occasionally, some child would defend his actions by saying, "My daddy told me that if anyone hit me first I was to hit back." I discovered that those who were taught this were the ones who were always "hitting back first."

Youth

This is the stage which can be labeled "In Search of Self." Peers are highly influential. Physical appearance is prominent. Wanting to be like others, the young person is vulnerable to the latest fads in clothing, hairstyles, and entertainment. This may be a period of self-preoccupation. Love may still be at the level of "I-need-and-I-want" stage. At this stage a person may expect to receive something in return, but not in every case. He is growing toward greater maturity in his liberality. He may lack a consistent and conscious philosophy or belief system about who to love and why.

Adult

Adults have the capacity to see from another's point of view. They, therefore, have a choice of whether they will meet their own needs or that of another. As adults mature, they are more able to think from another's point of view, decide what another would enjoy, and then do for another what he would appreciate.

YOUR TURN: Where are you on your journey? You may be at an adult level or still at the preschool level. Intelligence is necessary, but it is not sufficient for your attainment of maturity in loving others. Preschoolers and children are limited by their level of thinking. Youth and adults are basically at the highest level of thinking. They can think abstractly and from another's point of view, but they may behave as preschoolers or children in their motives for loving others.

Early Childhood

Do you merely imitate the loving actions which you see others doing without knowing why?

Do you love others because of the attention you get for your performance or behavior?

Are you self-centered (thinking from you own point of view without putting yourself in another's place to consider his needs or wants)?

Is seeing believing? Do you form your opinions of others on externals without considering another's needs?

Childhood

Do you love others to get their attention? To get some kind of reward or favor?

Do you believe in "getting even" when someone mistreats you? (When someone hits or hurts you, you hit or hurt back.)

Youth

Do you conform to the ways your peer group shows love?

Do you lack a conscious philosophy (a reason) for loving others?

Adult

Do you love those who love you?

Do you love those whom you know will return your love?

Do you love your spouse, boyfriend (girlfriend), best friend, children unconditionally—no matter what, no strings attached?

Do you love others solely because you can meet a need which they have?

Do you love those who are not easy to love (who may even reject your love)?

Do you love your enemies?

Do you accept and love all people no matter where they are on life's journey?

Do you see each person as made in the image of God, one whom God loves and for whom Jesus lived and died?

LOVE'S GUIDING PRINCIPLE

My husband brings coffee to me in bed every morning, a habit he acquired after all our children left the nest. *You* might say he is pampering me. *I* say he is showing love. He knows how much I enjoy and appreciate this, and he gets pleasure out of making me happy. (With a smile in his eyes and a chuckle in his voice, he tells me, however, that he does it in self-defense.) I know he is practicing what Jesus taught when He said, "Therefore whatever you want others to do for you, do so for them, for this is the Law and the Prophets" (Matt. 7:12). Fred does not want coffee in bed; so for me to practice this teaching (the Golden Rule), I need to do something for Fred which he enjoys, such as baking him a cake. For Fred, there are only two kinds of cake—good and better. Practicing this principle is not always easy because you are forced to think from another's point of view.

When you buy a wedding gift for someone, do you think what you would enjoy, or do you think what the other person would enjoy? Would you prefer to receive a gift of something you prefer or something another prefers? Notice the action of the young woman who goes to the bridal registry in a local department to discover what her friend has selected for wedding gifts. She sees the word *pewter*. "How could anyone want pewter, it is so dull? I will buy her a *silver* goblet." Self-centered or empathetic?

During a long meeting in which several panel members had spoken and another was about to begin, I observed a man in a wheelchair approach the microphone. He began by saying, "I know that you would like to stand and relax before we continue." He who could not stand understood and met the needs of those who could.

Raymond, who had been in prison for several years, had just signed up to have a visitor. My husband works with a prison fellowship and agreed to visit Raymond. He was the only person other than family on Raymond's list of visitors, and Raymond's family did not visit him. To me, one night a week seemed like a lot of time to give to one person—a total stranger.

Raymond calls our home about once a month. The last time he called he said, "Everybody needs somebody who cares, or else you feel like a nobody." Fred has been that somebody who has helped Raymond feel like somebody—somebody worthy of love and care. Raymond reports that he now is that somebody to several of the inmates who seem to have nobody.

Mature love meets the needs of another. The motive is not to get but to give. Have you experienced this truth, "It is more blessed to give than to receive" (Acts 20:35)? Accompanied by three colleagues, I was driving from Kentucky to Arkansas to attend a professional meeting. Suddenly we felt the bump, bump, bump which alerts you that a tire is going flat. Pulling over to the shoulder of the road, I noticed a car with two young men pulling over just behind us. "We have been watching your tire go down and were just waiting for it to get flat so that we could help you." What a relief! I would have tried to change the tire, but I never had changed one before. When the young men finished, I called them by name and tried to pay them. When they would accept no pay, I asked for their addresses. They must have anticipated that I would try to repay them; so they declined saying, "We just wanted to help you." Left almost speechless, I responded that I would just have to pass the kindness on to strangers in need whom I would find along the road.

"If you loved me, you would pick me up on time." "If you loved me, you would have my dinner cooked when I got home from work." "If you loved me, you would lose those extra pounds." "If you loved me, you would keep my car in good condition." All these statements put conditions on love. Mature love is unconditional. You love another because he or she is a person of value and worth—not because they conform to your wants, needs, and expectations.

If you are experiencing difficulty in a relationship, take a look at your expectations which may be conditional. Are you placing demands upon another which seem unreasonable to the other person? A sure way to change your friend's or spouse's attitude and behavior is to begin noticing the things which you appreciate. Discontinue fault-finding or nagging. If you can, ignore those things which annoy you. If you cannot, use the "I feel *(how you feel)* when you *(specify the behavior)*" statement. Be attentive. Give generous physical affection. Bestow acts of kindness. When you use your time to enhance a relationship, your life becomes more exciting and rewarding. Just stand back and watch attitudes change and love blossom.

Love My Enemies?

Some people are easier to love than others. Those who are least easy to love may be those who need our love the most. We are all children of God by creation. People are for loving. People are not for hurting. God loves us all. God wants the best for all of us. That is why Jesus taught: "I say to you, love your enemies, and pray for those who perse-cute you in order that you may be sons of your Father who is in heav-en. . . . For if you love those who love you, what reward have you? . . . Therefore you are to be perfect as your heavenly Father is perfect" (Matt. 5:44-48). The word *perfect* does not mean "without spot or blemish." It means becoming more Godlike in mind and character or getting good at being you—the one and only you God made.

A city was shocked by the disappearance of an elderly woman known for her generosity and charitable work in behalf of the many transients who live on the streets of the city. While engaged in this work, she was seized and brutally murdered by one she was dedicated to helping. Her son, a priest, felt no need to avenge his mother's death. He felt great sorrow for one who felt he had to commit such a deed. I believe that this young priest, like Jesus, said, "Father, forgive him, for he knew not what he did." Such compassion.

As you grow toward maturity, you do not think of others as ene-mies. You think of each person as made in the image of God. Each needs to feel valuable and worthwhile. Each needs to feel loved. Each is a person for whom Christ died.

Jesus said that loving deeds which you do for others are done to Him. When you feed the hungry, give drink to the thirsty, clothe the naked, visit the sick, or visit in prison—you did it to Him (see Matt. 25:36).

YOUR TURN: Search your own need to love and be loved. What do other people do for you which makes you feel loved? Or how do you like for others to treat you?

How can you make the most important person in you life feel loved?

Think of someone you know who has the most need for love? What can you do to help this person feel loved?

How can you show people whose lives you touch daily that they are loved?

Now, for the difficult one, who are your enemies? How can you show love to these? How will you show love to these?

4

ENJOY AND APPRECIATE OTHERS

"Beloved, let us love one another, for love is from God; and every one who loves is born of God and knows God" (1 John 4:7).

A principal smiles at a kindergarten teacher
   and twenty-five children profit.
A customer notices how thoughtful a postal worker is
   and every customer of the day benefits.
And so it is that . . .
   When you smile at another,
     the smile lives on.
   When you notice another,
     the good will thrives.
   When you bring delight to another,
     the enjoyment continues.
   When you appreciate someone,
     that someone passes it on.

Do you like for people to smile at you? To notice you or acknowledge your presence in a kind manner? Do you like for people to call you by name when they greet you or talk with you? Do you like for people to look into your eyes with gentleness? We are human and each of us wants to be treated as a person of value and worth. When we are treated this way, we feel appreciated. So as you consider ways that you can enjoy and appreciate others, ask yourself how you like to be treated. Then treat people this way even if they do not treat you as you wish to be treated.

Galileo said, "You cannot teach a man anything. You can only help him discover it within himself." So I am asking you to look within yourself for answers to how you can help others feel valuable and worthwhile. Within you are rich resources which you can use to assist you in getting along with others, working with others, and appreciating others. When something appreciates, it goes up in value. How exciting to give yourself to the opportunity and privilege of appreciating people!

YOUR TURN: To begin with, close your eyes for a moment and reminisce. Take a journey back into time and bring to your conscious memory those things which others did to or for you which brought you joy. When you have reveled in these memories, make a list of them. As a result of knowing what you appreciated, what can you do to enjoy and appreciate people so that others can experience joy?

"GREAT OAKS FROM TINY ACORNS GROW."

On a preaching engagement in North Carolina, a Texas minister visited a mountain craft shop to purchase a gift to take home to his wife. In the front of the store were displayed exquisite wooden sculptures of animals native to the area. So impressed was the minister with the intricate detail that he questioned the sculptor who was at work in the rear of the shop. "Tell me, Sir, how can you carve this carefully detailed miniature dog out of a block of wood?"

The sculptor paused, deliberated, and casually answered, "Well, what I do is just cut away everything that doesn't look like a dog."

Can you, like this sculptor, see deep within each person a person greater than he is, greater than the person thinks he is? Can you see within that which God made this one able to become? Within each person lies the potential for greatness. Ours is the grand opportunity of helping every person discover what he can become.

An elderly woman confided, "You know, I would have treated that young boy who delivered my milk a whole lot differently if I had known he was going to become a respected world evangelist." We, too, have missed opportunities to affirm others. We can start right now using our blessed opportunities to treat everyone as if they had the potential for greatness. For every person has the potential to become the wonderfully able person God made him or her to be.

During my early years living in a church parsonage, I became acquainted with many ministers who stayed in our home while they led revivals in the churches my father pastored. My father pastored five churches at one time—called a circuit. He served four churches on a half-time basis. He preached twice on Sunday morning, at night, and in the afternoon each fifth Sunday. Among these gracious ministers who stayed for a week in our home was a young woman named Lea Joyner. She and my father exchanged pulpits throughout the years. As a pioneer woman minister, Lea was appointed to a mission church in a deprived area. She joyfully accepted the challenge.

When she preached, I had dreams of becoming a preacher just like Lea. From my earliest association with her, I knew she loved me, God loved me, and God had something special for me to do. Every Sunday School paper, card, or leaflet I received was carefully saved. Surely I would use these when I began my ministry. As a child I felt called to preach. Later, I felt called to teach.

A few years ago while leading a conference in a church in Shreveport, Louisiana, I mentioned the name Lea Joyner. Sharing with these preschool teachers the importance of the impressionable early years, I spoke of this woman's influence on my young life.

A teacher whose father I remembered as a friend of my father, quickly responded, "Sybil, did you know Dr. Joyner was murdered recently?"

What a shock! I wanted to know the details. She was murdered by one whom she was trying to help. What a tragedy! But my thoughts went back to the time when Jesus, her Lord, was crucified by those He came to help.

Sometime later I meet a man from Louisiana and discovered that we both had lived in Downsville, Louisiana. He asked me if I remembered Julia Beth Holman. "Oh, yes. When my father was appointed to a circuit near Downsville, we lived with her family for a few weeks. She was like my big sister. Then the conversation turned to my need to know more about Lea Joyner. He did not know the information I wanted, but he promised to get it.

Just as I was writing this chapter, I received in the mail a book, *Standing in the Gap* by Harry Hale, Jr., on the life and ministry of Dr. Lea Joyner from my long-time friend Julia Beth. Soon thereafter, a letter arrived explaining how triumph came from this tragedy. God works in mysterious ways to provide our every need!

God used this beautiful life over many years to touch the multitudes. To accommodate the thousands of friends she had loved and helped, the funeral was held in the Monroe Civic Center. Prior to the memorial service, two thousand mourners signed the guest books in the church sanctuary where Lea's body lay. The small mission where she began was the prelude to a thriving church. Southside United Methodist Church is now Lea Joyner Memorial United Methodist Church. Following her death, the state Legislature approved a resolution which required the Federal Department of Transportation to change the name of the Louisville Avenue Bridge to the Lea Joyner Bridge. The city council renamed the Monroe Civic Center Expressway the Lea Joyner Memorial Expressway. Etched in stone, wood, and steel are the words *Lea Joyner*. But the greatest monuments to her life are etched in the hearts and lives of people she touched for God. I am one among the many of those.

YOUR TURN: Who has seen greatness in you (seen more in you than you did) and encouraged you to blossom? Take a moment to think of five persons who have most influenced your life. Recall what each did to give you a vision of what you could become. Include someone from your childhood. your youth? your adult years? God is the Source of your potential—what you can become. You can help a person discover his possibilities. As you enjoy and appreciate people, you communicate to them their value and worth. You can help them think more highly of themselves, that is, develop a healthy self-esteem. This is what you can do. The poet Goethe said it this way, "Treat people as if they were what they ought to be and you help them to become what they are capable of being."

THE SELF-FULFILLING PROPHECY

What you think, you become. The writer of Proverbs says, "As he thinks within himself, so is he" (23:7). Let us see how you can affect how another thinks about himself.

As a college student I read reports of research findings on how what a teacher expects of a pupil affects his intellectual development. The idea is that if a teacher expects a child to be bright, he becomes bright. If she expects him to succeed, he does succeed.

In Greek mythology the story is told of Pygmalion, a sculptor, who fashioned a beautiful ivory statue of his ultimate woman. In response to Pygmalion's prayers, Galatea, the statue, was brought to life by the goddess Aphrodite.

In George Bernard Shaw's summary of his work *Pygmalion* is the statement, "The difference between a lady and a flower girl is not how she behaves, but how she's treated." The Broadway musical *My Fair Lady* carries this theme. The professor takes on the task of teaching a flower girl of the street how to talk and behave like a lady. He treats her like a lady and she becomes a lady—his fair lady.

Treatment Does Made a Difference

In all our relationships we are involved in "treating" people. How you treat a person affects what the person thinks he can become and ultimately what he does become. This same effect on behavior was found to be true with animals. Experimenters were told that the animals in their research study were genetically inferior. When the animals were treated in an inferior manner, they performed more poorly. When experimenters believed that their animal subjects were genetically superior, they treated the animals as superior subjects, and the animals performed accordingly. There were no genetic differences between the two groups of animals. If animals expected to be bright did indeed become bright, would the same be true of children whose teachers expected them to be bright?

In an elementary school the teachers in grades one through six were given the names of those children who would show dramatic intellectual growth according to alleged standardized test results. Actually, the children's names were selected at random. But when teachers thought that these late bloomers were going to blossom, they did. The teachers communicated their expectancy through their facial expressions, body language, conversation, and touch.

You, too, can expect great things from others. You can develop the marvelous ability to see in every person the potential for becoming a beautiful, caring, competent, compassionate being. By your actions and your words, you can communicate your expectancy. Then stand back and watch them blossom.

Caterpillers Are Destined to Become Butterflies

I wanted personally to test the effect of a teacher's influence on a child's ability to blossom. I selected Carolyn, a student in my kindergarten class. I had taught her older brother, but since that time there were three other children. A beautiful, dark-eyed girl, she could not speak distinctly; she was shy and had difficulty looking you in the eyes. I decided I would pay special attention to Carolyn. She would know I expected her to become a beautiful, outgoing person. I noticed, noticed, noticed her actions throughout the day and said such things as "I enjoy watching you paint, Carolyn." At group time, I would mention something she had done during free-choice activity time. The time finally came when Carolyn had the confidence to walk up by my side, stand in front of the group arranged in a semicircle, and hold up the picture which she had painted. I could ask her to tell me about her picture, and she could say a few words in front of the group.

Later she joined in as we played a game. A blindfolded child would sit in a chair and pretend to be It. Carolyn would take her turn standing behind the blindfolded child. She would knock on his back as the song directed. When the question "Who's that knocking at my door?" was sung, Carolyn would sing, "It is I"—a three-word solo. Then the blindfolded child would guess who.

Carolyn enjoyed being with me so much that she began arriving earlier than the other children. I enjoyed this special time with her, and I encouraged her to help me prepare the room and the snacks. At the end of the year, Carolyn had indeed changed from a shy, withdrawn, almost nontalking young girl to an overt, sparkling child who could look you in the eye and speak distinctly. Amazing metamorphosis!

At the end of the school year, Carolyn and her mother came to my house bearing a gift—a beautiful antique-framed mirror. On the brown paper which sealed the back of the mirror were these words: "For a most memorable year. Love, Carolyn." When I feel the need to be affirmed, I just turn the mirror side toward the wall, so I can see the words on the back.

When I attend church services or meetings, I try to think about who most needs a friendly pat on the back or a word of encouragement. As I am arriving or leaving, I purposely select someone to talk to. One Sunday while singing in the choir, I noticed a sad look on the face of a young mother. I said to myself, "When the service is over, I will go to her."

After the service, I walked quickly to her and said, "I just wanted to say what a joy it is for me to see you and your lovely family here today." She broke down and shared with me that she had missed Sunday School because she was having a problem with her strong-willed daughter (about seven years of age). During the week I received a thank-you note telling me how much it meant to have someone who cared enough to listen when she so needed to talk.

A few months ago I received a long letter from a mother telling me about her now grown-up daughter. She was a recent cover girl on a national magazine. Her mother, in a glowing statement said, "And she is just as beautiful and wholesome as she appears in the picture."

Our desire is for everyone to live out their greatness, to fulfill their destiny, and to develop their God-given potential. How sad is the plight of one so generously endowed by God to come to the end of life realizing he has used such a little part of it.

PEOPLE NEED PEOPLE

Hurting People

All around are hurting people—shackled with heavy burdens. Think of three people whose path you cross daily. Behind each face, smiling, solemn, or sad, what pain lies beneath? In my rainbow of friends, these are the pains which have been shared with me:

> a daughter is in a medical facility being treated by a psychiatrist,
> a friend, son, daughter, mother, father, brother, sister, or relative is in the throes of a difficult divorce,
> a loved one is dying of a terminal disease
> a widowed mother has her adult son committed for treatment of alcohol abuse,

a teenage child is on drugs,
a relative or friend is pregnant and unmarried,
an unwed daughter is living with a man,
a son or friend has declared or been identified as a homosexual,
a friend has been terminated or resigned under pressure from
        work,
a family has gone bankrupt,
a son or daughter has run away, their whereabouts unknown,
a child has been diagnosed as mentally handicapped,
a person is in the anguish of depression,
a young adult struggling with the various demands of reentry
        into college to prepare for a new career,
a single parent (male or female) copes with the discomfort of
        sharing a child with the other parent.

Joyful People

All around are people experiencing joyful things. Something new:
spouse,
baby,
house,
furniture,
clothes,
achievement or attainment,
job,
boyfriend (girlfriend),
relative,
restored to health,
promoted in business,
elected to new positions.

These are those who need you to enjoy and appreciate them. We are admonished to "Rejoice with those who rejoice, and weep with those who weep" (Rom. 12:15).

Is it easier for you to weep with people or to rejoice with people? At times I have found it easier to weep than to rejoice. "Why?" I ask myself. Because I do not envy the position of the one with whom I weep, but I often envy the position of the one with whom I rejoice. On many occasions when attending the celebration of a new house, I would so envy the beautifully decorated house that I would confess afterward to my husband, "I do not need to go to another open house—all I do is envy and feel sorry for myself because I do not have one equally as beautiful." Then I would quickly say to myself, "I am a reluctant learner but my goal is to be able to say as Paul, 'I have learned to be content in whatever circumstances I am'" (Phil. 4:11). **YOUR TURN:** Look back at the lists of hurting people and joyful people. Decide which hurt or joy which you have heard about recently. You may want to make a list and write by each how you can show your loving care to these.

Select someone who needs you most. Determine to expect great things from this person. Decide how you will communicate your expectations of the following idea. "I see in you far greater than you see in yourself. God has placed in you such wonderful potential. I want to see you become all God made you able to become." Keep a daily diary of what you do and say and the results. Share your plan with a person you can trust. Share the continuing results. Watch your prayer being answered.

For Starters

1. Notice people. Acknowledge their presence. Look into their eyes. Smile. Greet them with encouraging words. Get away from the "How are you?"—"I am fine" ritual. Try something different—maybe, "Make for yourself a wonderful day!"

2. Call a person by name. Your name represents who you are. Call a person's name in love so as to communicate, "You are valuable and worthwhile to me." After years of teaching student teachers and observing them during their practice teaching, I came upon a new idea about using a child's name. One morning for three hours I observed a student teacher teaching kindergarten children. I heard Charles's name (called at times when he misbehaved) about twenty-five times. When I met with the student teacher I said as tactfully as I could, "Do you know how many times you called Charles's name for misbehaving?" She did not know. She was shocked when I said, "Twenty-five." I asked, "I wonder what Charles is beginning to think about himself?"

YOUR TURN: What do you think Charles is learning about himself? I wanted Charles to know he was valuable and worthwhile, able, and capable. The student teacher wanted the same thing. So I suggested that she notice anything Charles did which even approached being appropriate and use his name to thank and affirm him. I suggested that if she did this, she could watch him grow and blossom. He will no longer need to be a "bad" boy to get attention because he will be getting attention for the right things.

Expect a child to do what's right, and he will seldom disappoint you. Call a child's (person's) name often when you are acknowledging you are happy to be in his presence or when you are affirming or thanking him for helpful behaviors.

3. Listen when a person speaks. I sometimes give my mind a jog by saying, "Sybil, set your margins, and punch your *clear* button (typewriter terminology), so you will focus only on what is being said." When you listen, you are giving away a part of yourself.

4. Give physical affection generously and appropriately. Reach out and touch, pat another's arm or shoulder a few times gently, give a hug, touch cheek to cheek, and greet one another with a holy kiss (Rom. 16:16) or with a kiss of love (1 Pet. 5:14).

5. Affirm people. Support and encourage people with positive comments and gestures. Saying "I love you" will have more meaning when backed up by acts of kindness. Let your talk become your walk. Some things you may choose to do are:

- write a letter or a note when such is unexpected
- put love notes in your spouse's luggage when he or she leaves for a trip
- leave notes for the spouse at home to find (under the pillow, on the mirror)
- send flowers or other remembrances
- present yourself at home as you would in public (that will cheer you and anyone else around)
- take someone on a break or out to eat. Say "Tell me about you . . ."
- express interest and enthusiasm when you greet someone
- go through a day without saying anything critical
- mention to your spouse or friend how pretty/handsome she or he is

- do something to assist someone
- phone someone who needs a message of cheer
- compliment another's handiwork or achievement
- send a thoughtful gift
- overlook faults
- talk to people about the good things of your day—and listen to theirs
- add your list of ideas for the little things you can do to say "I appreciate you."

6. Use pleasant words. "Pleasant words are a honeycomb, sweet to the soul and healing to the bones" (Prov. 16:24).

7. Respect people—the highest of God's creations. People are not for hurting. People are not for using.

YOUR TURN: Think of some actions and some words which will communicate "I enjoy knowing/being with you and appreciate you" to:

1. your spouse (or boyfriend, girlfriend, best friend)
2. a relative
3. a person with whom you work
4. a neighbor (someone who needs your help)
5. an acquaintance
6. anyone I meet
7. a classmate or fellow club member
8. a fellow church member
9. an enemy or one who is your problem person (one who "rubs" you the wrong way)

BOOMERANG!

The love which you send out comes back. When I was attempting to think of a Bible verse with this same truth, I thought of "Whatever a man sows, this he will also reap" (Gal. 6:7). Another verse came to mind: "Cast your bread on the surface of the waters, for you will find it after many days" (Eccl. 11:1). I asked people to tell me what this verse meant. What was the literal meaning "bread on the surface of the waters" that would come back? Most thought the verse had to do with generosity but did not know what these words really meant. I went to a Bible for an explanation. One explanation was that *bread* meant *grain*. The grain was sent out in ships across the water to be sold. In verse 2 a further explanation calls upon the person to divide the portion and not send all in one ship in the event of misfortune—natural disaster. Whether the meaning has to do with what comes back from the sale of grain or what comes back to you as a result of what you give, the meaning is clear—what we send out comes back.

Feeling challenged by a young man who told me about how he had given a sizeable amount of money to a secretary who was having difficulty paying bills, I, too, wanted to learn how to be generous. He mentioned that each time he was generous, the money came back to him in unusual ways. My motive was not to get paid back with money. I just wanted to show appreciation by giving what I possessed and giving a part of me. But just when I had made a commitment to be generous, I made a stunning discovery.

During an illness of my husband, I was forced to assume responsibility for balancing the checkbook. While studying the statement from the bank, I discovered a bank draft for fifty dollars for which I could not account. I looked at several statements and found this same bank draft. I assumed that this was my husband's insurance payment, until my husband said that he paid the annual premium by personal check. So I wrote the insurance company and discovered that due to a clerical error, the insurance company had been deducting this monthly amount from the bank since December of 1979 to pay for another policyholder's coverage who happened to have an identical name. In the letter was a refund for $4,308.66 that represented the total amount incorrectly withdrawn and a check for $958.79, which represented the compounded interest earned on the amount. I do not want to suggest giving with a selfish motive of expecting something in return, but I always know that what is sent out comes back with interest.

Experience a remarkable aliveness. Enjoy and appreciate people, and people will enjoy and appreciate you.

5

BE YOURSELF

"Distributing to each one individually just as He wills" (1 Cor. 12:11).

As a child did you dress up in mother's or daddy's clothes and hobble or slide around in their shoes? Did you at some time want to be one of those community helpers whose work was identified by a uniform—the fire fighter, police officer, doctor, nurse, or mail carrier?

You, like I, wanted to be just like the important people in our lives. We learned by imitation or by the models or examples we had.

As a young person I wanted to be just like my friend Nell Rose who lived in our home during our senior year because her parents had to move to a nearby town. My daddy frequently reminded me, "Sybil, you are talking like Nell Rose again." He was saying, "Be yourself"; but I was slow to receive the message.

In high school I wanted to be just like my chemistry teacher, Mrs. Ford. To me she was so smart to be able to teach something which was so difficult for me to understand. When I selected my engagement ring, I asked for a pearl instead of diamond. Why? Mrs. Ford wore one.

I also wanted to be like my high school principal, H. H. McKinney, who taught me history. Mr. McKinney had an informal club of students whom he expected to succeed in life. As he taught my history class, he would occasionally mention students by numbers he had assigned and tell about their achievements. One day he handed me a small rectangular piece of notebook paper which had in bold print these words, "A quitter never wins, and a winner never quits." Underneath was the numeral *eleven*. I was "number 11" in his club. On each of the four corners was one of these words: scholarship, loyalty, character, honesty. These words have inspired me: (1) to be self-disciplined (do what has to be done when it has to be done), (2) to be dedicated to the truth, (3) to delay gratification until responsible tasks are performed, and (4) to be faithful to my God. H. H. McKinney practiced what he taught.

His untimely death by cancer prevented me from telling him personally how much his life enhanced mine. Later, I was able to get in touch with the widow of H. H. McKinney and share with her how her husband's life had blessed mine.

YOUR TURN: Who did you want to be like when you were growing up? How did you want to be like these people? What a relief to discover that you do not have to be like anyone else. You can be encouraged and inspired by others who use their abilities effectively. While you can learn from others, you can also learn how to use your abilities in your own special way. Hopefully, you will discover, earlier than I did, that God made you different from all the rest for a distinct purpose. You are very special.

GOD MADE YOU UNIQUE

You can relish this truth: God made you one of a kind. You are a Designer's original. There never has been, nor is, nor ever shall be a person just like you. So celebrate your uniqueness. Join with the psalmist who sang this praise to His maker:

"For Thou didst form my inner parts;
Thou didst weave me in my mother's womb.
I will give thanks to Thee, for I
    am fearfully and wonderfully made;
Wonderful are Thy works,
And my soul knows it very well" (Ps. 139:13-14).

You are one of God's wonderful works—a unique creation. Tell yourself that right now and never forget it. The words on a popular poster say it this way, "God didn't make no junk."

YOUR TURN: On a sheet of paper or in your notebook, write the ways in which God made you unique—different from everyone else in the whole world. How has God wonderfully made your body? Your mind? Your spirit?

GOD HAS A PLAN FOR YOU

God must have something very special for you to do since He made you one of a kind. I believe as Jeremiah did that God knew you before you were born, and He has a unique purpose for your life.

"Before I formed you in the womb,
          I knew you,
And before you were born
          I consecrated you;
I have appointed you a prophet
          to the nations" (Jer. 1:5).

You can discover what God has appointed you to do, what plans He has for you. Whether you are a young person at work or in college, a homemaker, or an employed adult, retired, living alone, confined, and unable to get around, God still has a purpose, a useful purpose for your life. As Jeremiah continued, " 'I know the plans that I have for you,' declares the Lord, 'plans for welfare and not for calamity to give you a future and a hope' " (Jer. 29:11). A ninety-three-year-old mother questioned why God left her on earth instead of her son-in-law. She answered her own question. "He must have something left for me to do. I can comfort my daughter."

God sent you into the world with a special mission to accomplish. You can do some things better than anyone else in the world. You can touch some lives in a way no other person can. The worthiness of your mission and your success in accomplishing it are measured only by God. You are called to touch their lives. God will put them in your path, or He will direct you to them. You will seek no recognition nor praise. Your joy is found in the accomplishment or fulfillment of your mission.

YOUR TURN: What do you think is God's plan for you at the present time? At some future time?

RECOGNIZE YOUR GIFTS

Think of what you are best able to do, and the gifts (talents) which you have. Remember, gifts or talents do not come fully grown. Talents are at least 90 percent hard work.

Look at this list of gifts and circle those which you believe you have: encouraging, comforting, sharing, sewing, cooking, typing, singing, drawing, peacemaking, conversing, listening, affirming others, noticing others, caring for children, helping the sick, gardening, growing flowers, speaking, building, and planning. Add other gifts to the list.

When you love yourself, you are free to be yourself and to use your unique gifts. You do not need to compare your gifts to another. To compare would be unfair.

ALL PEOPLE ARE GIFTED

People do not possess the same gifts, but all are gifted and can use their gifts in a special way. Paul writes about spiritual gifts in 1 Corinthians 12:4-11. Paul refers to people who are followers of Christ as members of a whole body. Each person is a vital part of the body. When members use their gifts wisely, the whole body profits. When we neglect using our gifts, the whole body suffers. As an eye would be foolish to say to a hand, "I have no need of you," no one member can say to another, "The body does not need you." Each person is needed (vv. 12-22). Also, notice that the members whom we think less honorable will have more abundant honor. God gives more abundant honor to the member which lacks. How comforting to know that what we consider small gifts, God can greatly honor (vv. 23-24).

Small Gifts

God honors what Richard Foster calls "the ministry of small things." In the Bible is recorded the story of an ordinary woman named Dorcas, a seamstress, who was known for her deeds of kindness and love. She sewed garments for the poor. In Luke 3:10-14 we are asked to use our small gifts—to share what we have and to show kindness.

In my young adult years, I had the privilege of discovering, enlisting, and training teachers for the preschool departments. I had a dear friend in the church named Marie, a radiant Christian, who was warm, personal, and talkative. I approached her: "Marie, I believe you would be a wonderful teacher of preschoolers. You are so kind, gentle, and caring." Marie was shocked. "Why, I can't teach. You know I can't talk before a group."

"Marie, you can talk easily with me and to your friends in everyday-life situations. And that's what teaching young children is, talking to them as they play (work) in everyday-life situations. Marie accepted the challenge. I can see her now, sitting on the floor with an opened Bible in her lap, looking into the eyes of a child and talking in soft, gentle, caring words. I can see her showing the picture of Jesus and the children in the Bible. I can hear her saying: "This is a picture of Jesus. Jesus loves you; and I love you, too."

Marie gained confidence as she practiced her gift of loving the children. In my mind is stored a beautiful picture of Marie leaving the church to visit in the homes of the preschoolers. She took with her a Bible which had appropriate pictures for preschoolers, a record player, and a recording. Once inside a house, she would sit on the living room floor with the child, play the recording, and say to the child: "Jenny, we will play this recording next Sunday morning at church. I hope you will come." Marie discovered her gifts and her calling.

Large Gifts

While most people feel led to use their gifts in a ministry of small things, some will be called to tasks of courage involving risk just as Esther was. You perhaps will want to read the whole story in the brief Book of Esther in the Bible. Esther risked her life to go before the king in behalf of her people. And as Esther was challenged, so are we. "Who knowest whether thou art come to the kingdom for such a time as this?" (Esther 4:14, KJV).

Mother Teresa has given her life to the ministry of small things—helping the poor and needy. Her name is now a household word. Her small deeds multiplied many time have brought widespread recognition and influence.

NO COMPETITION

Since God made you with unique gifts, you no longer feel the need to compete with others who are also uniquely gifted. You can spend your energies competing with yourself—that is, improving your own abilities.

I used to feel shy singing, speaking, writing, or playing the piano or organ, leading a conference, or teaching a class, for fear that someone in the audience could do better than I. Now if I have a responsibility to play the piano, for example, during a worship service, I fulfill my responsibilities as I am able. (I am not there to perform, but to assist in worship.) When I am to speak I do not concern myself with the fact that in the audience may be those who can speak better than I. My desire is to do what I have been asked to do in the way God best made me able to do it. I do not have to speak nor lead a conference like anyone else, I can do it my way.

I want you to feel confident using your gifts. Your gifts do not have to be better than anyone else's for you to be able to use them.

A noted conference leader had just led a conference for hundreds of people using this title, "How to Lead a Conference." As the people left the room, a woman said, "If that's the way you lead a conference, I will never be able to lead one." She was overwhelmed by the super expertise of this conference leader's dramatic style. I reassured her. "You don't have to lead a conference like he does to be an effective conference leader. You can develop your own style." Enjoy and accept the challenge of perfecting your own skills and abilities. *Enjoy the comfort and freedom of being yourself.*

YOUR TURN: Write a plan for developing your unique abilities and skills. Write some specific things to do and a time schedule for doing them.

6

RADIATE JOY

"These things we write, so that our joy may be made complete" (1 John 1:4).

YOUR TURN: To get in touch with how you feel about yourself, note the statements which are true . When you complete the chapter, read these statements again and see how your responses have changed.

I sometimes feel that no one understands me.

All I do is work.

I get very little positive affirmation.

I have problems relating to people.

I wish I could be more assertive—speak up and express myself.

I sometimes find myself discussing the faults of others (gossiping).

I find myself doing "good" things for others (feeling that I should) and hating every minute of it.

I need to find some time for me.

I cannot accept criticism without getting my feelings hurt.

I have to be right.

I just love to tell others what to do (my own way seems better than their way).

I enjoy catching another in a mistake.

I seldom look for positive things in others or share complimentary words.

I want what I want no matter what.

If my supervisor were to call me to the office, I would know I'd done something wrong.

I sometimes feel people are saying things behind my back.

I wish I could (add your own words for something you wish *you* could do) like (think of someone who does this particular thing well).

If you found yourself needing to check several of the preceding statements, this chapter is especially for you. I hear you saying that you are leading a lackluster life—one that is joyless. I pray that your joy may be full. Work with me as we discover fullness of joy. Let us begin by thinking about a big subject—"the kingdom of heaven"—and we are still discussing joy. People talk about *heaven*, but how many can tell you what the Bible says about heaven and what they believe about the *kingdom of heaven*?

YOUR TURN: Write in one sentence what you think *the kingdom of heaven* is. Be honest. Tell it like it is. When you finish this chapter, look at what you have written and see if you want to change your sentence. Richard Foster in his struggle to understand the kingdom of God shares this insight: "Jesus was not trying to teach us how to get into heaven, but He was trying to teach how to get heaven into you." Heaven is a destination, but the goal of the Christian is life in the kingdom of God. Jesus wants you to experience fullness of life now. John the Baptist fulfilling his mission to "Make ready the way of the Lord" preached "the kingdom of heaven is at hand" (Matt. 3:2-3). In what we call the Lord's Prayer, Jesus taught His disciples how to pray using these words: "Thy kingdom come. Thy will be done, On earth as it is in heaven" (Matt. 6:10). Note the words *on earth*. We are to *live* the kingdom life. The kingdom of God is in the here and now, as well as in the hereafter.

The word *salvation* means "health" or "wholeness." We become whole or complete when we become as humble and trusting before God as little children. Notice Jesus' answer to the disciples who asked, "Who then is greatest in the kingdom of heaven?" Jesus responded by calling a child to stand next to Him. "Truly I say to you, unless you are converted and become like children, you shall not enter the kingdom of heaven. Whoever then humbles himself as this child, he is the greatest in the kingdom of heaven. And whoever receives one such child in My name receives Me" (Matt. 18:1-5).

On another occasion, the disciples rebuked the parents who brought their children to Jesus so that He could touch them and pray. Jesus taught them saying: "Let the children alone, and do not hinder them from coming to Me; for the kingdom of heaven belongs to such as these" (Matt. 19:14).

When your heart is open to God's will for your life and you seek it with all your heart, you shall surely find it. The relationship of children to their parents is an earthly illustration of our relationship to the Father—dependent, trusting that the Father who is all-wise knows our needs and will lovingly meet our every need in keeping with our best interest. Jesus said, "But seek for His kingdom, and these things [food, clothing—physical needs] shall be added to you. Do not be afraid, little flock, for your Father has chosen gladly to give you the kingdom" (Luke 12:31-32).

Let us become as children and both ask and trust that God will give us the kingdom. Jesus asks that we give our possessions to those in need and, thus, lay up treasures in heaven. "For where your treasure is, there will your heart be also" (Luke 12:34). God did not promise health, wealth, and prosperity. He promised joy and strength and the power of His comforting presence to enable us to live fully in the midst of good times, as well as hard times—times of trial, suffering, disappointment, and the challenges which each age and stage bring.

FULLY AND JOYFULLY ALIVE

"Stone walls do not a prison make,
    Nor Iron bars a cage."[1]

Your spirit can survive and thrive and be joyous even when imprisoned. Many people today feel trapped—caught in a seemingly impossible circumstance. God, being your helper, you can have joy and can pass it on to others. No matter how difficult things may seem, tell yourself, "I choose to have joy, and I choose to give joy to others."

Dietrich Bonhoeffer, a great Christian leader, while confined in a German prison expressed through poetry his struggle of soul in a poem "Who Am I?" He admitted that his captors told him that he bore the "days of misfortune equable, smilingly, proudly, like one accustomed to win." He wondered if what they said was true or if he was a hypocrite. He felt restless, like a bird in a cage, struggling for breath, and yearning to see the color of flowers and to hear the voices of birds.

He thirsted for words of kindness and neighborliness and felt weary and empty at praying and thinking.

Perhaps you, too, have experienced such loneliness and emptiness in your life, or, felt imprisoned in your own household, your workplace, or church, or lived with circumstances over which you had no control.

Note the ending of Bonhoeffer's poem: "Whoever I am, Thou knowest, O God, I am Thine!"[2] When you pour out your soul to God, you can come to the same comforting conclusion. In the book *Ask Me to Dance* Bruce Larson describes a life-changing event. At the end of World War II in Germany while he was waiting his return to the States, he noticed a handful of men who were not just marking time— they had a sense of fulfillment and a future hope. Being led by the regimental chaplain, a Southern Baptist minister, these men were engaged in a small Bible study group. The witness of these men changed him. While kneeling in a bombed-out apartment building in Stuttgart, Germany, where his outfit was stationed, Larson told Jesus Christ He could have his life to do with it as He would. He admitted that he did not know all that was involved, but he gave Jesus all his life, whatever that meant. This began for him an adventure which he is still on. In 1972 Bruce Larson, a Presbyterian clergyman, with a B.D. from Princeton and an M.A. in psychology from Boston University wrote the book *Ask Me to Dance*. In demand as a speaker and conference leader, he has authored many other books. A monument to radiant, joy-filled living, he states that the church is full of people of faith asking us to teach them to " dance." People hunger for a deeper walk with Christ that helps them dance for joy—a dance of the heart filled with happiness.

A HEART DANCING WITH JOY

A few months ago one of the many transient people who live on the Nashville streets visited our church which is several miles from downtown. Well do I remember him attending the services on Sunday and Wednesday night carrying a large duffle bag containing all he needed for his present existence. How grateful I was that the people accepted him, unkempt and needy as he was. Feeling safe, secure, and loved in our fellowship, he continued coming for several weeks. Then we saw him no more. Recently one Sunday morning, our pastor announced that he had received a letter from the young man. Expressing thanks for the Christian love shown him when he was at his lowest and worst, the man enclosed a check for $600 to be used for the exciting building program which was being promoted at the time he attended. He was an Ivy League college graduate, but he had become addicted to alcohol and had lost it all. He was now genuinely converted, back at work, and living a joyous new life through Jesus Christ.

"DANCE"—LEAP FOR JOY!

Years ago I read the book *Dancing at My Funeral* by Maxie Dunnam. Dunnam had a soul-changing experience. Admittedly, he had no technical knowledge of dancing nor was "the dance" in his culture. He made this distinction. Funerals are about death, and dancing is about life. In order to live, Dunnam had to die to resentment, guilt, self-hate, and remorse—those things that weighted him down. He dances when he has the courage to resist forces that would bury him. He dances in the face of tragedy because he trusts God to help him be the victor, not the victim. Life is for dancing (truly living) the victorious, joyful life.

When you use your God-given abilities—your life as He directs and keep His commandments, you will hear Him say, "Well done, good and faithful slave; . . . enter into the joy of your master" (Matt. 25:21).

"Let us lay aside every encumbrance [things that weight you down], and the sin which so easily entangles us, and let us run with endurance the race that is set before us, fixing our eyes on Jesus, the author and perfecter of faith, who for the joy set before Him endured the cross, despising the shame, and has sat down at the right hand of the throne of God" (Heb. 12:1-2).

YOUR TURN: Reread the verses above. Note in particular the part about "lay aside every encumbrance" and the part about "joy." Laying aside these weights precedes joy. Now you are ready to have a funeral to bring those things which prevent you from being whole—healed, saved, cured, and well. Search your soul to discover those weights which are burdening you—holding you down, keeping you

from feeling the comforting, satisfying, fulfilling joy which Jesus came
for you to possess. In your notebook or on a sheet of paper, draw a
box. In the box list those things you have thought of.

Look at your list. Can you choose to bury these—put them out of
sight and out of mind—and set your mind and affections on things of
eternal importance? If so, draw a lid on the box and close it forever.
Now can you dance (rejoice in the heart) at their funeral?

"Christ in you, the hope of glory" (Col. 1:27)

What a joy is ours to be an instrument through whom God works.
God has given us the tasks of proclaiming and teaching, so "we may
present every man perfect in Christ Jesus" (Col. 1:28, KJV), or "complete in Christ."

You like Paul, an apostle of Jesus Christ, can say, "For this purpose
also I labor, striving according to His power, which mightily works
within me" (Col. 1:29). A paraphrase of the words is: "This is my
work, and I can do it only because of Christ's mighty energy at work
within me" (TLB).

The word *perfect* means whole. Jesus Christ came to make your life
and mine whole. The word *salvation* came from a word meaning
"health" or "wholeness." What does *whole* mean? Have you ever sung
the hymn "Whiter than Snow"? The first stanza begins, "Lord Jesus, I
long to be perfectly whole." When you sing words in hymns, do you
think about what they mean? And if you do not know what they
mean, do you hasten to find out what they mean? How much time
have I wasted that was set aside for worship because I sang or said
words without asking what they meant or without thinking about
what they meant. Worship and praise are true thoughts lifted *to God*.

A woman who was hemorrhaging believed that she would be made
"whole" if she could but touch the hem of Jesus' garment. To her Jesus
said, "Daughter, be of good comfort; thy faith hath made thee whole"
(Matt. 9:20-21, KJV) or "your faith has made you well."

On another occasion recorded in Luke 7:36-50, Jesus called attention to a woman of the city who was a sinner. The Pharisees were
concerned that Jesus was letting this sort of woman touch Him. Yet,
Jesus let her wash His feet with her tears and wipe them with her hair,

let her kiss His feet, and anoint them with perfume. Because she expressed her great love, Jesus said, "Your sins have been forgiven. . . . Your faith has saved you; go in peace" (vv. 48,50).

Have you danced the dance of wholeness? In Acts 3:1-10 is the story of Peter healing a crippled man at the gate of the Temple. The healed man entered the Temple with Peter and John "walking and leaping and praising God" (v. 8).

Wholeness brings meaning and joy to life and is cause for celebration. Meaning and joy can be felt even in times of pain, sorrow, hurt, frustration, loss, and setbacks.

Even in the midst of death, Jesus spoke of life. He did not go immediately when notified of his friend Lazarus's sickness. Lazarus had been dead for four days when Jesus arrived. Jesus called in a loud voice, "Lazarus, come forth." Lazarus came forth, and the burial wrapping was removed from his body. Jesus demonstrated what He had said to Martha, "I am the resurrection and the life; he who believes in Me shall live even if he dies and everyone who lives and believes in Me shall never die" (John 11:25-26) and Jesus asked Martha, "Do you believe this?" (v. 26). Can you as Martha proclaim, "Yes, Lord; I have believed that You are the Christ, the Son of God" (v. 27)?

CONSIDER IT ALL JOY WHEN YOU HAVE TRIALS

All people at times face difficult circumstances.The difference in the way people respond is a matter of attitude. You can choose to radiate joy because you are fully confident in God's goodness and His desire for your very best. You can choose to be filled with bitterness and hate or forgiveness and love. Our faith gives meaning to our experience. When we are made whole, His love dwells in us; and we are healed in body, mind, and spirit.

Triumph or Tragedy?

On a Sunday afternoon a man and his son invited the neighbors' son to go for an outing on the lake. The neighbor's son was drowning; and in an effort to save the boy, both lives were lost.

Losing her only son in a boat accident, Margie Riley chose to love another's son. She did not resort to bitterness or self-pity, rather she gave herself in love to others. In losing her life to others, she found it for herself. Through the years this saintly woman has taught adults in Sunday School, and as church librarian she has encouraged many to read helpful books. She has brought joy to countless people who have come and gone from the church and the community. My husband was her pastor three decades ago. Our younger son was the beneficiary of her motherly love. Both she and her dear husband, Mr. Jay, a respected deacon and county clerk, became "grandparents" to Mark.

Through the years Margie Riley has been affectionately called Job (the one for whom a book in the Bible is named). Her body is an incubator for skin cancers—she has had these from her head to her feet, even on her eyelids. She jokingly laughs about her famous feet which have been literally on display at medical conventions.

While returning from a trip one summer, my husband and I were privileged to visit Margie in Gainesville, Texas. She told us about a recent surgical procedure in which she lost the sight in one eye.

Her sight loss does not prevent her from doing what she needs to do; she just has to put forth more effort. My most recent letter from her asks me to excuse the typo errors which occur now with greater frequency. Undaunted, Margie appropriates the words in 2 Corinthians 4:8, "We are troubled on every side, yet not distressed; we are perplexed, but not in despair" (KJV).

A young man from a respected Christian family felt called to preach; he completed his seminary training and served in several positions of ministry. Well loved and popular as a preacher, this young man with a wife, a preschooler, and a new baby was involved in a criminal act. What a tragedy! What a waste of talent and influence! As a wife and a mother, my first thoughts were: *I wonder how his mother and father must feel, how his wife must feel, how his children will feel.* The young man's family thought about giving up their church responsibilities. But their pastor and fellow church members encouraged them not to; the family members returned to their responsibilities. Theirs was the choice of triumph or defeat. They chose to triumph over tragedy. This father who has suffered over the wrongdoing of his son is mellow, tenderhearted, and empathetic with others who also suffer. The experience itself was not good, but what is happening as a result is working for good. Christian people had an opportunity to suffer with (comfort) this family. Crushed by this shocking revelation and an unbelievable string of events, this family was brought together to support each other and to lean heavily upon the Divine Comforter. They still love their son, they always will. They do not understand. They are grieved by his behavior, but they love him. That is Godlike. God loves us with an everlasting love. While we were sinners, He gave His life for us. "But for the grace of God, there go I."

Success or Failure

Success is not at the top of the corporate ladder, not humane acclaim over an earthly accomplishment, not the attainment of a commanding salary, not being a household name, not being promoted to a higher position, nor holding the highest educational degrees. Some who have achieved these heights of earthly status do not have joy. To them life is a grind, a treadmill or an *un*merry-go-round from which they scream, "Stop, let me off." True success is measured by the assurance that you are at peace with your Maker and fully involved in His will for your life. You are instruments of His love in a materialistic and pleasure-driven world. Success is knowing that you are getting good at being the one-and-only you. There is no greater success story than the One which resides inside the person fully committed to living the abundant life which comes through faith in Jesus Christ and the sustaining and enabling power which He alone can give.

Recently, my husband shared with me an exciting book he had discovered. Never intending to be published, Isobel M. Garver filled dozens of private journals spanning thirty-five years. Following her long struggle with cancer and inevitable death, her husband shared the brilliant galaxy of her dialogue with God in a book entitled *Stars in the Night* which reflects the hope she held during life's darkest moments. Today God is still using her influence to touch the lives of others and shed light upon an otherwise dark path.

YOUR TURN: How can you have joy during time of hardships? How can God use your trying times to help you? When physical healing is not possible and we are appointed to die, we can be assured of soul healing. Our dance is not one of leaping with our feet; but it is one of

leaping with our spirit, knowing that God's love is within us and surrounds us. The psalmist sang, "His favor is for a lifetime; Weeping
may last for the night, But a shout of joy comes in the morning" (Ps.
30:5).

William James in his book *A Variety of Religious Experiences* de-
fined conversion as "the process, gradual or sudden, whereby a person
who is previously unhappy, inferior or wrong, becomes consciously
superior, happy and right." What a transformation! Jesus can create in
you just such a change. He came that we "might have life, and might
have it abundantly" (John 10:10).

Jesus *changed* my life and *is changing* my life. There was a time in
my life when I was controlled by fear. I felt unhappy, inferior, and
unworthy. I sought release from the oppression through the words of
great hymns and through Scriptures. A hymn, "O for a Thousand
Tongues to Sing," soothed me with these words:

     "Jesus, the name that calms my fears,

     . . . .

     He sets the prisoner free."

A Scripture which comforted me was: "God hath not given us the
spirit of fear; but of power, and of love, and of a sound mind" (2 Tim.
1:7, KJV). *Fear* is translated *timidity* in the *New American Standard
Bible.*

The joy of wholeness in Jesus Christ is recognizable. When you are
whole, you radiate joy. Jesus did not fit the notion in His day of what a
holy man was. He ate with tax collectors and sinners, talked with a
woman of bad reputation, healed on the sabbath, and praised a helpful
Samaritan (despised by the Jews). He went about doing good. He was
no respecter of persons. To Jesus all people were worth living and
dying for. As Paul states, "There is neither Jew nor Greek, there is
neither slave nor free man, there is neither male nor female; for you
are all one in Christ Jesus" (Gal. 3:28).

Francis of Assisi was so joyous and authentic that the people called
him God's merrymaker. He was noted for his "holy hilarity"—the
kind of merrymaking which occurs when a father welcomes home his
wayward (prodigal) son or a person comes home to God. Can you
make merry because another who was wayward returns home, or do

you feel like the elder brother—jealous and filled with self-pity?
YOUR TURN: Read the story of the Prodigal Son (Luke 15:11-32).
Describe each of the three persons in the story: the younger son (vv.
11-21); the father (vv. 11-12,20-24,31-32); the older son (vv. 25-32).
Which of these experiences joy with abandon? In what ways are you
like any of the three? Why is the older brother robbed of his joy?

My heart's desire is that you will be free to be yourself, to enjoy
God, and to help free others to discover and use their gifts. May you
be free of all those things—bitterness, resentment, self-pity, self-hate,
envy, lust, greed, and covetousness—which rob you of your joy. Let
no one or no thing rob you of your joy. The choice is yours.

[1]Richard Lovelace, *To Althea from Prison.*

[2]Dietrich Bonhoeffer, *Letters and Papers from Prison*, rev. ed., ed. Eberhard Bethge
(New York: Macmillan, 1967), pp. 188-89.

[3]Bruce Larson, *Ask Me to Dance* (Waco, Tex.: Word, 1972)

7

BE GENUINE

"O Lord, who may abide in Thy tent? Who may dwell on Thy holy hill? He who walks with integrity, and works righteousness, And speaks truth in his heart" (Ps. 15:1-2).

Did you ever play "Let's Pretend"? When you overhear young children at play, you often hear, "Play like you are the mommy, and I am the daddy." Each will put on Mommy's or Daddy's shoes, hat, and clothes. And then one will begin to "cook" or "care for the baby," and another will go "buy groceries."

Sometimes we grow to be adults still enamored with the game "Let's Pretend." How many hats do you wear? You may be a different person as a friend than you are as a spouse, parent, child, manager, or employee. Do you sometimes feel that you are "playing" a role, pretending to be someone you really are not?

LET ME INTRODUCE MYSELF

How can you be genuine unless you first discover who you are? Ask yourself: "Who am I?" Consider this a special time to learn about a most important person! Tell me about a most fascinating person—you.

YOUR TURN: Write three things you would like for people to know about you as a child. As a young person. As an adult. John Powell who wrote the book "*Why Am I Afraid to Tell You Who I Am?*" told a friend the title of his latest book. The friend inquired, "Do you want an answer to your question?" And, of course, John Powell wanted an answer. The friend answered, "I am afraid to tell you who I am, because, if I tell you who I am, you may not like who I am, and it's all that I have." Do you have this same fear? Are you one of those who tries to hide who you really are and project an image of what you would like to be? T. S. Eliot called this universal deception the "art of being 'hollow men.' " G. K. Chesterson said it this way, "We are masters of the art of deception, pretending to be what we are not in the hopes that no one will discover the real person we are." Can you be honest with yourself? Shakespeare said:

> "To thine own self be true,
>   And it must follow, as the night the day,
>   Thou canst not then be false to any man."

WEARING MASKS

YOUR TURN: What masks are you wearing? On a sheet of paper, head one column NOT ME and another ME. Be honest with yourself. List the images you would like to project and the image which is real.

NOT ME

What I wish others "saw" in me.

ME

Will the real (Insert your name) please stand up?

Now try to think from another's point of view. What images do you think people have of you: at work (employee), or at home (spouse, parent, child), in the neighborhood, other.

We really want to be real. Who among us wants to be phony or counterfeit? Wearing masks, acting roles, and playing games are our way, often quite unconsciously, of protecting ourselves. When we have playacted or pretended for many years, we find it difficult to distinguish between the real and make-believe self. As you and I travel side by side on the road to self-discovery and what is real, let us ask God continuously for insight and wisdom. "God, force us to become just who we are—genuine, real, authentic."

On your soul-searching journey to discovering who you really are, take some relaxing, refreshing rest stops.

Rest Stop

I enjoy the book *The Velveteen Rabbit*, a fictional story about self-understanding, acceptance, and love. Skin Horse, the oldest toy in the nursery and well worn for all the loving he has received, chats with the toy rabbit. The velveteen rabbit asks, "What's REAL? . . . Does it mean having things that buzz inside you and a stick-out handle?"

"Real isn't how you are made," said the Skin Horse. "It's a thing that happens to you. When a child loves you for a long, long time, not just to play with, but REALLY loves you, then you become Real. . . . It doesn't happen all at once," said the Skin Horse. "You become. It takes a long time. . . . Generally, by the time you are Real, most of your hair has been loved off, and your eyes drop out and you get loose in the joints and very shabby. But these things don't matter at all, because once you are Real you can't be ugly, except to people who don't understand."

Jess Lair, in the book *I Ain't Well But I Sure Am Better*, says that it is vital to have five friends—people who like us just the way we are, who accept us "as is," who do not judge us, who do not try to change us, and who listen and share with us regularly. A friend is one who radiates a welcome when he or she sees us coming, and we send forth the same glad welcome when we see our friends approaching. We plan time to be together because we enjoy each other's presence. As we allow ourselves to become transparent, open, and honest, only then do we discover who we really are in the reflection of the mirror of the other person.

When you go to a good counselor, psychologist, or psychiatrist, you get help when you are able to reveal yourself completely. You are free to be you without fear of rejection because you will not be judged. This person does not seek to control, dominate, or judge you. Rather the helping person desires to help you become self-disciplined—able to make wise choices for yourself. When you get your honest thoughts outside yourself in the presence of one you trust, you can more ably gain insight and make wiser decisions.

A trusted friend to whom you can bare your soul can be this helping person. When I first read Jess Lair's suggestion, I could not think of five persons with whom I would share my honest thoughts and feelings. Listening to others bare their souls is easier for me than baring mine.

"Life is primarily a matter of relationships." Only through relationships with others do we come to know who we really are. God has made us both to need and to be needed by others. No longer can you say to the person in the other end of the boat, "I'm glad the leak is in your end of the boat." We are colonized on the spaceship earth, and what happens on one side of the earth affects those on the other side. Each of us has abilities—different abilities and abilities in different degrees. We are all needed to cooperatively meet the needs of those who live with us. Without people helping people, we all suffer. During any period of my life, what I am is largely determined by the people who love me and the people I love. The greatest gift I can receive or give is a love which accepts, does not judge, and expects no repayment except the freedom and joy of honesty and togetherness.

YOUR TURN: Pretend that this page is a mirror. Take a good look at yourself. What do you see? Behind the face what do you see? Before you share yourself with a friend, write your honest thoughts in your notebook or on a sheet of paper

Right now, this is what I am really like: This is what I really think: This is what I really feel: This is what I really love: Now how do you feel? Better? How did you feel as you were baring your soul? (One meaning of the word *bare* means "without clothes"—"nude." You feel undressed when you take off your masks and expose what lies beneath.)

Now think of one person who can be your trusted friend. Write the name on your paper. Take one step at a time and begin to share in natural moments of conversation those things which are important to you. You may want to keep a diary "On Becoming REAL."

GETTING IN TOUCH WITH YOUR ROOTS

Who has a greater influence on us than those upon whom we are most dependent during our impressionable earliest years? Try to retrieve from your mind's file the messages which you received from your parents or the most important people in your life.

When I look back to those early years I hear myself constantly saying, "May I . . . ?" As an adult I catch myself still asking permission. Just today I slipped up again asking permission. As my husband and I waited for a slow elevator, I asked, "Let me walk the stairs. I have been sitting a lot today." I am the person I allow myself to be. As a responsible person in my own right, I can now make my own decisions. You may find some of the early messages dictated by parents or teachers onto your tapes still playing and urging you to do as you are told.

Another message I received as a child which I have reevaluated is: "Anything worth doing is worth doing right." What I have discovered is that some things I do are more important than other things I do. I do not need to make *A's* on everything. I have to decide what has the highest priority. By virtue of priority, some tasks deserve only *B* work, others *C* and so on.

"Follow the rule," and "Do as I say and don't ask why," are other early messages that I received. As an adult, I must question each rule to know if following it is right or wrong. To be accountable for my own actions I must not blindly obey those who would tell me what to do. I am accountable to God for my own behavior.

"Don't walk on the grass" was a rule well ingrained within me. I have to tell myself many times that it is OK to walk on some grass. The tickling, spongy feeling of walking barefoot on the grass is relaxing and exhilarating.

YOUR TURN: Think for a few minutes about the "messages" you received as a child. You may have heard the messages or you may have felt them through the impressions you received. Then consider if this message is still an appropriate guide for your behavior. As the days go by, you may find yourself remembering other messages which you will want to list as you search to discover who you really are.On a sheet of paper or in your notebook, make a list, using the following headings:

Messages I Received and What I Think About Them Now.

THE GIANT STEP

Now take a giant step—an adult— step in the direction of self-discovery. When I was working on my doctorate, one of the most painful tasks I encountered was coming to grips with what I believed about the most important questions of life. Both in philosophy and in counseling courses, I had to state what I believed about human beings, their moral nature, and the meaning of life. Indeed it was a struggle of soul to discover *my* beliefs—not those passed down from my parents, my school teachers, and my church teachers. Some of the big questions are listed next. Search your own soul for *your* answers (honest answers), not what you have heard said nor read, but what you consciously, knowingly believe.

1. What is the most important thing in life?
2. What is the purpose of life?
3. Who is ultimately important? Why?
4. What is worth living for? Dying for?
5. If you gave something of importance, what would it be?
6. What is your philosophy of life (your belief about God, people, others, and the world—how each of these relates)?
7. Am I my brother's keeper?
8. Am I my brother's brother (sister)?
9. What is my first duty to God? to myself? and others?
10. What is life?

Now that you have read these tough questions and written some answers, you will find that thoughts on the subject will pervade your mind. You will continue to seek more satisfying answers. Seek God's wisdom through prayer, read the Bible, and study commentaries for additional information. Also, record other questions of eternal importance.

Sometimes we are like Alice in Wonderland who asked, "Would you tell me, please which way I ought to go from here?"

The Cheshire Puss answered, "That depends a good deal on where you want to get to."

Alice said that she didn't much care where she was going.

The Cat replied, "Then it doesn't matter which way you go."

Sometimes we are so busy traveling that we do not question where we are going. Some of your answers to the previous questions may encourage you to ask which way you ought to go. Hopefully, you will find your way in the direction of discovering more and more about what you genuinely believe is important.

If you are beginning to feel a little uneasy, consider these feelings as "growing pains." When you meet a new idea, you can ignore it, consider it, and choose to dismiss it, or you can choose to consider its merits. If you do the latter, you will try to fit the idea in with what you already know.

Of the many books I read, I find few, if any, that I can accept in full.

In most books I read, however, I find something which I can use (apply to my life). May you savor the experience of growing pains as you develop wisdom and grow in knowledge of the truth which sets you free to become genuinely you.

FREE TO BE YOU

Are you free to be you—the unique person God made you able to be? Or, are you on your way? Explain.

Controlled from Without or Within?

Are you a person in your own right? Are you your own person? Can you say that no one or no organization or group owns you? Getting good at being *you* means learning to take responsibility for yourself, your actions, your attitudes, and your choices.

Do you think for yourself? Search for the truth? God has given you freedom of will—a tremendous stewardship. You have the freedom to make choices.

God does not make choices for you. He has equipped you with a marvelous mind. You are made in His image—rational and intelligent. You are able and capable. You can take care of yourself. You can solve problems. God has made you to seek fellowship with Him and with others He has made. Life, then, is primarily a matter of relationships with God, with others, and with yourself. You are accountable to God for the choices you make. Choose to be genuine—to become fully you.

THIS IS YOUR LIFE

Now that you have gotten in touch with your roots and grappled with what life is about, look at where you are on your journey of life. **YOUR TURN:** Draw a line across a sheet of paper. Above the line write "My Life Span." At the beginning of the line write birth. At the end write death. On the line place a dot to show where you are presently. Put an (x) to note important happenings in your life. Below the (x) label the happening on a diagonal line (as in *birth* and *death*).

What do you want to accomplish before you die? Put a check mark on the line when you expect to accomplish this and then label it on a diagonal line.

When we measure the present and the past in terms of the ultimate, life takes on a different perspective. How do I want to spend my time, energies, and talents in light of eternity? What really matters anyhow?

ACCEPTING YOURSELF

Pretending to be something you are not, wearing masks, requires energy, time, and juggling. Wearing a mask is something like telling a lie. When you tell a lie, you have to continue lying to cover up the first one. To save face you have to keep pretending and trying to remember which mask you are wearing.

To be who you really are is to feel wonderfully comfortable with yourself. You accept who you are where you are. You are free to forget the games people play and to occupy your body, mind, and strength in productive ways. You can just be you.

I used to get so angry at people who did not understand that I was driving the best I could. When they would blow their horns at me and made ugly gestures or mouth hateful words, I would fight back in like manner. How sweet it is now to smile, send my love, and mouth these words, "If you really knew me, you would like me!"

8

LISTENING TO YOURSELF AND OTHERS

"Finally, . . . whatever is true, . . . let your mind dwell on
these things" (Phil. 4:8).

LISTEN TO YOURSELF

Most of the day you spend talking to yourself. If you get lost in your
work which requires your total attention, you stop talking to yourself
and perform your work. Much of your work, such as cleaning house,
mowing the lawn, or filling the car with gas is done on cruise control
or automatic. You do not really have to think very much about what
you are doing. So your mind starts thinking about other things.

Driving to and from work is a wonderful time to chat with yourself—to plan, pray, and make decisions. Your thoughts are safe inside
you. You talk to yourself about many things which you do not say to
others. These are your hidden messages. They remain hidden until
you choose to reveal them.

If you really want to become acquainted with yourself, write what
you really think—get your thoughts outside of you—look at them objectively and determine what is really bothering you.

Years ago I heard this story. An employee was reprimanded by his
boss. Unable to talk back to his boss, he went home to his lovely wife
who had worked hard to prepare a delicious meal. The potatoes were
not done enough. The steak was too done, and nothing was warm
enough. The wife turned to their young son who looked just like his
father and told him to sit up straight and eat every bite of food on his
plate whether he liked it or not. The little boy was last seen as he
slammed the kitchen door. He was on his way to find the dog. Woe be
unto the dog! As each person displaces his anger, the real messages

inside remain concealed. Much of what we think, we keep to ourselves. On the other hand, some people will give you a piece of their
mind—and you wonder if they have any left.

Listen to your thoughts—the words which come to your mind which
you do not say aloud. When you listen to what you say to yourself,
you are really listening to your heart. You think about what you will
do to cope with the problems you are facing. What thoughts occupy
your mind?

These are examples of untrue thoughts people sometimes say:

I'm a failure.

I can't enjoy my work.

I can't lose weight.

I can't get a job.

I can't quit smoking (drinking, gambling, overeating, overspend-
ing, procrastinating).

I can't exercise every day.

Nobody loves me.

I'm just no good.

I can't get up in the morning.

I just can't get going on my work.

I can't get organized.

I can't help but feel lonely.

I can't deny myself. (I must have what I want when I want it.)

I can't stand it when I am criticized.

I can't stand it when she talks to me that way.

I can't speak up when I really want to.

I can't keep from saying what think. (I have hoof-in-mouth
disease.)

I can't stop being a workaholic.

I can't help getting angry (enraged, infuriated, irritated) when he .
. .

I can't stop acting like a martyr—"Poor me."

I simply can't get my work done.

I'm dumb.

Now, for each of the untrue statements which you have thought or
are now thinking, write a *true* statement. Tell yourself the truth about

the matter. Here are some examples.

Untrue Statement You Say to Yourself:

I can't enjoy my work.

Talk Back to Yourself. Tell yourself the truth:

No work is 100 percent enjoyable. Some of my work is stressful. Some people I work with are difficult. I have some problems at work. Make a list. I have a choice. I can choose to enjoy my work, or I can choose to find work which I can enjoy. My problems are not insurmountable. I can choose to control how I feel about my work and the people I work with. I cannot change people, *but I can change me.*

Untrue Statement You Say to Yourself:

I can't assert myself (express my thoughts, feelings, desires).

Talk Back to Yourself. Tell yourself the truth:

I do at times express my thoughts, feelings, and desires. I will choose to express myself when I feel I need to. I will do so tactfully. I will court opportunities to express helpful thoughts.

Untrue Statement You Say to Yourself:

I can't lose weight.

Talk Back to Yourself. Tell yourself the truth:

I can lose weight if I choose to. I can choose to eat right and to eat less. I can choose to exercise (walk, run) on a daily basis. I can choose to eat slowly and think about how wonderful the food tastes. I can enjoy talking with others while I eat. I can tell myself that being fat is not me.

I understand having a weight problem. I have had one. I have lost a thousand pounds as Erma Bombeck says. During my husband's long-term depression, I told myself I had to do something for me, something for fun—eating was fun. My reward for working so hard was to indulge in a midnight snack of butter cookies and milk or some decadent dessert. I chose food for my reward. I chose to be fat. When I saw myself in family photographs, in videotapes, and in the mirror, I thought, *This is not me. I do not want to live the rest of my life looking like this.* I asked God to help me get rid of my ungodly fat, and I chose to eat right and less and to walk briskly 30 minutes a day. Fortunately, my husband shared my interest in developing a healthy body. We meet at a mall on our way home from work and enjoy a 30-minute walk. This is a time for talking about things other than work, planning our schedules, and visiting with other walkers who have become our friends. How rewarding to hear my friends say: "I'm seeing less and less of you." "You look great!" "Skinny Sybil." Those are words I thought I would never hear again.

Untrue Statement You Say to Yourself:

I can't be happy with my spouse.

Talk Back to Yourself. Tell Yourself the Truth:

I choose to be happy with my spouse. I do not like some things my spouse does. He or she probably does not like some things I do. I will treat my spouse the way I would like to be treated.

THE TRUTH IS: "LIFE IS NOT EASY. LIFE IS TOUGH."

Life is filled with pain, separation, loss, stress, discomfort, disease, illness, and aloneness. The irony, however, is that when you recognize this truth and accept it, you have realistic expectations. You take charge of your life. You handle problems as opportunities. You get on with living. Your attitude makes the difference.

Two Myths

Life should be all pleasure. If you just love the Lord and commit your life to Him, you will be healthy, prosperous, and only wonderful things will come your way. The Christian is spared pain, discomfort, misfortune.

Not true.

I should have what I want when I want it. I deserve it. I cannot wait; I need instant gratification. The world revolves around me. I know how to manipulate people to get what I want. I will do what I have to do to get what I want.

The truth is that self-discipline is important to mental and spiritual health. You can wait. You can learn that you are important and other people are important. Your rights end where another's rights begin. People are not for *using*.

LISTEN TO YOURSELF

What do you want most of all in life? Do you want to thrust your-self wholeheartedly into becoming the best you possible? Then seek to discipline your life. Do your work (and do it well) when it has to be done. Choose not to indulge yourself. You can wait for some things in order to achieve your ultimate purpose. Do not become a slave to your unreasonable desires. You can say *no* to yourself when *no* is in your best interest. Expect the best of yourself.

An unhappy, miserable wife confided that she did not even like her husband. "He is so dogmatic, so inflexible. He doesn't understand me or the children. His expectations are unreal. We will never be enough for him."

When she did the activity using the two categories *Untrue Thoughts* and *True Thoughts*, the wife decided that she did have a problem. She could not change her husband. She could change herself—her atti-tude. Instead of fighting back and nagging, she found herself saying, "You know I hadn't thought of it that way." She began to notice every-thing positive she could about her husband, every little attempt he made toward showing he cared for her and the children. "You know," she said, "I really intended to just change my attitude, and when I changed—he changed. He is much less dogmatic and much more thoughtful."

LET GO OF YOUR NEGATIVE THOUGHTS

Push negative thoughts outside your mind. Savor the freedom of being cleaned and purged from these. Replace them with love. Knock that chip off the shoulder. Such relief, such calm! Such stillness when the burden is lifted. Away with defensiveness—defending why you are the way you are. When you say you can't help it or someone else is to blame just say to yourself: "I choose to listen to me, to respect my thoughts. I will talk back to me. Nothing can keep me from the grand purpose which God ordained for me. Onward, upward with diligence. When I tell myself the truth about me, I can get on with living. No more self-hate, no more hate for others, no more animosity or bitter-ness—these cancerous, infectious feelings weight me down when God wants me to soar. I forgive all the wrongs that have been done me. I believe in the marvelous abilities which God has so abundantly given me. What I think I believe. What I believe I live."

TURNING POINT

When you stop carrying the excess baggage of putting yourself down, finding fault with others, allowing others to determine your feelings, you are free to grow and become the real you. Eleanor Roosevelt is credited with saying, "No one can make you feel inferior without your consent." You can choose how you will let others treat you. You can choose how you will let others influence you. You can choose not to let others upset you.

Just a few days ago I was attempting to follow my husband's car to a gasoline station. He made a left-hand turn, and I was caught with the traffic light. I found myself obstructing the traffic coming from my right which had to turn to the left around me. Just as I was attempting to back up to get out of the way, a man whom I know quite well but who did not recognize me felt inconvenienced (to put it mildly). As he wheeled around my car, I noticed his body language—grimaced face, lips uttering familiar four-letter expletives. In days past I would have gotten angry at him and would probably have gestured in like manner. How wonderful to know that I can choose not to get upset. I will not own his anger. I will love him no matter what. I forgive him. I will never call it to his attention.

LOOK INTO THE MIRROR OF CHILDHOOD

Handsome, competent, well-groomed, intelligent, but defensive, dogmatic, bemeaning, highly critical—this can happen when a person has a low view of who he is. He knows that his self-image is poor, and he still blames it on his dad who always put him down.

A child learns who he is from the significant others in his life. How a child feels about himself is learned in the early years. During the first and most important years of life, a child learns to trust or not to trust the person on whom he depends. When a parent meets a child's need upon demand during this year, the child learns to trust himself to make his needs known, and to trust another to meet his own needs. Learning to trust, he becomes more independent the next year.

During the second and third years of life, the critical task to learn is independence—the "I can do it myself" feeling. If parents do for the child what he can do for himself, he learns to depend upon others. He does not become a person in his own right. To become a person in his own right, he needs to make choices and live with his choice (accept the natural consequences of his choice). A child should be able to choose between two foods, two drinks, two garments—both of which are appropriate. He should be able to choose to share or not to share. To force a child to give up to another is not sharing and does not teach sharing. It teaches power—that big people can make you do things you do not want to do. Parents can well learn to offer choices to young children. For instance, when the family is enjoying a snack with visitors and the child's bedtime is approaching, you might say: "You may choose to have one cookie and then go to bed, or you may choose to go to bed without a cookie." Or, when your child does not want to share with a visiting child, "You may choose to take the truck to your room and play with it alone, or you may choose to let Sean have a turn." The child then learns to accept responsibility for his choice. A child may learn, given the choice, that sharing can be more fun than playing alone. Mainly, a child learns how to share by seeing the important people in his life sharing what they have. The burden of the teaching is on the adult. A person with a good self-image feels competent making wise choices in his best interest and in the interest of others who are affected by his choices.

By age three a child learns that he is the center of the world, or that he is important, and others are also important. If parents give in to a child's unreasonable demands during the first years, the child learns how to work people to get what she wants. A mother takes her young child to the grocery store. At first the mother says *no* to her screaming child who wants the cereal with the toy inside, but she later gives in to stop the embarrassing situation. She has just taught her child that if she screams loud enough and long enough, she can get what she wants. She learns how to manipulate others. A person who has a good self-image does not need to manipulate others. She can be open in relationships. She wants what is good for herself and for others.

During the later preschool years is the time to help children develop responsibility—the feeling that "I can help. I can think of ways to help (I can take the initiative)." Children need to share in the work necessary for meeting their basic needs: food, shelter, clothing, recreation. If parents always do the work, the child grows up feeling that everyone should serve him. A six-year-old can help vacuum the floor, feed the pet, make up the bed, put toys away. An eight-year-old can start learning to do laundry and ironing. And he can feel great about being able to do what adults do. Most parents want their children to grow up and to become self-controlled. Yet they sometimes feel so insecure that they find their only worth in living through their children. Little do they know that they are denying the child by preventing him from learning responsibility. A working mother of a college graduate, living at home, feels that she must iron his shirts. Then she complains about how hard she has to work. A working mother of a college student and a high school student still irons their clothes. She is "earning" their love. They are learning that others are to wait upon them. A mother of a 50-year-old bachelor still goes to clean his house which is only a few blocks away. She thinks she is helping.

Children who are allowed to receive the natural consequences of their choices are on their way to self- control. If a child does not get up in the morning when his alarm goes off, the natural consequence may be that he misses school. "Oh," you say, "if I let him miss school, he will do it every day."

No, not if he has to stay in his room all day and go to school without an excuse from his parents. Not if he has to tell the teacher the reason for his absence—he overslept.

Parents make the mistake of always excusing a child's behavior or blaming circumstances. If the child is irritable, someone says she's tired, hungry, sleepy, or bored. Often parents are responsible for a child's irritable behavior—neglecting the schedule for eating and rest. Sometimes parents set children up for failure. They let them eat between meals and punish them for not eating at mealtime. Parents need to take responsibility for their behavior and help the child learn to take responsibility also. "You can choose to eat while the family eats, or you may choose to sit with us while we eat. When the family is finished eating, the food will be put away." You may be thinking: *Now I know why I am like I am. It is not my fault. My parents are to blame.* Your parents did the best they could. You are now an adult. You can no longer blame them. As an adult, you have a choice to change. It is never too late. People are very resilient—if they choose to be.

Children may feel indulged and expect others to be their servants, or they may feel exploited. Some of you may say, "My parents used me to make them look good. They wanted to make me a superkid in school and the hero on the ball field. I had no childhood." Parents who do not feel valuable and worthwhile try to get their value and worth from their children. Children need and want limits. Limits provide security. A child thinks, "When you set reasonable limits, I know you care about me." I never saw a happy child who was left to himself with no limits.

YOUR TURN: Look into the mirror of your early years. Did you learn to trust yourself—in your ability to get help when you needed it? Did you learn to trust others upon whom you depend? Did you learn to do things for yourself which you can do? Did you learn "I am able and capable"? Did you learn to make choices? Did you learn to consider what is best for you to do, keeping in mind the effect of your choices on others? Did you learn to be responsible? To do your share of what has to be done? Did you learn to feel valuable and worthwhile? A child's success in school, adolescence, marriage, and vocation can be predicted by age six.

Your personality—your expression of who you are and how you feel about yourself—is the key to success in relationships. If you learned you are valuable and worthwhile and that others are valuable and worthwhile, you respect yourself and others—you want the best for you and them. You live life fully and productively—wanting to make a difference.

THERE IS HOPE!

If you did not learn to trust, to be independent, to be responsible, if you did not learn to feel valuable and worthwhile, you can start right now. Tell yourself the truth about yourself. Accept responsibility now for your life. You are in charge. God has given you this stewardship. Start viewing life as one choice after another. What choices will you make today? Make of list of them. Consider your choices related to worktime and leisuretime. How will you use your money, express love to people, and exercise your mind, body, and spirit?

WHEN YOU LEARN TO LISTEN TO YOURSELF, YOU ARE IN THE BEST POSITION TO LISTEN TO OTHERS.

One evening as my husband backed the car out of the garage down the driveway into the street, I noticed a mound of something in the front yard. "Someone has been here," I exclaimed.

"Yes, I just *told* you that Cos brought us a load of mulch."

How often have you sat alongside someone who was talking to you, and you heard but did not listen? You were thinking your own thoughts. You even occasionally said "uh—huh" to make the person think you were listening. I have wasted a lot of time hearing tactfully and not listening.

As a child, my habitual response to my mother's request for me to do something was, "What?" I would be so absorbed with my playing that I could not tune in to her first words, and the last words did not give enough information. But before she could repeat what she said, I would remember all of it.

WHEN YOU DO NOT LISTEN TO OTHERS, YOU DISCOUNT THEM.

Discounting others is selling them short of their real worth. Listening is a matter of respect. While I was pressured with the deadline for this book, I was having coffee with two friends. One was sharing an experience of her early teens when she was embarrassed to sing for a group. Her mother had volunteered her for the job. A few moments later I asked, "Well, how did you do?"

"I just told you—my voice cracked, I was out of breath, and it was awful."

A young woman attended a weiner roast with her husband and became acquainted for the first time with many new men and women. She confided in me that she desperately wanted to remember the names of several of the women. But she felt so self-conscious wondering what they were thinking about her that she could not listen to what they were saying. She could not remember even a few new names.

LISTENING REQUIRES TAKING TURNS.

You take your turn talking. I listen. I take my turn talking. You listen. But does this ever happen to you? While the other person is talking, you are so engrossed in how you will respond that you are not tuned in to what is being said. When you get caught not listening, do you fake it (pretend you were listening), or are you honest and say: "I stopped listening. Would you repeat that, please?"

LISTENING IS A WAY TO GIVE YOURSELF AWAY

When you really listen, you give your time, your energy, your mind, your focused attention. You loan yourself to another. Listening is not something you are born knowing. You learn to listen.

Counselors and psychiatrists learn to listen nonjudgmentally. When you become another's judge, you cut off communication. When I talk to you, I want you to listen, not judge. A good listener listens so attentively that he can repeat what the other has said.

READY?

Listening is difficult. You may need to mentally review these guidelines before you practice listening to someone.
I will . . .

1. Take the initiative to listen (tune in).
2. Give focused attention.
3. Stop talking.
4. Remove distractions.
5. Allow emotion. (While I will be joyous over the other's good news and can hurt when another hurts, I will choose to maintain composure so that I *can* listen.
6. Allow silences. To pick up a conversation too soon may cut short another's comments. The purpose is to encourage the other to continue talking.

7. Withhold judgment. You can judge the effects of a person's actions, but you cannot judge his motive or reasons. Only God can judge the heart.

8. Be patient.

9. Keep confidences.

10. Avoid advice and problem solving.

God has made each of us accountable to Him for our choices. Making decisions for others robs persons of their God-given responsibility and makes them more dependent.

You can help a person discover options and consider the consequences.

GET SET

1. *Listen with your body.* Turn your body in the direction of the person talking, so you can look face-to-face. This communicates readiness and willingness. "I want to hear you." Assume a relaxed but alert posture. Say silently to yourself: "I will be attentive to this person's words and actions. I will attempt to receive the message."

2. *Listen with your eyes.* Eyes are the windows to the soul. Look into the eyes of the other with loving care. You can tell how another person is feeling and how he feels about himself by the look in his eyes. People who feel low self-worth have a difficult time looking into your eyes.

Even little children know how important the eyes are for listening. A favorite cartoon of mine shows the father sitting in his lounge chair reading his paper while his little boy is tugging on his arm and saying, "But Dad, you hafta listen with your eyes." You can show with your eyes you are interested in what the other person is saying.

Look at the body language or facial expressions, body position (slumped or upright). The eyes (fiery, tearful, still, moving, sad, happy). Notice how a person walks. Body language can exude confidence or fear, interest or disinterest. A brisk walk, shoulders erect, face smiling, eyes twinkling, outstretched hand, and firm handshake—these communicate confidence. Slumped shoulders, sloppy posture, downward look, weak handshake, taunt facial expression, dull or lifeless eyes communicate lack of confidence.

3. *Listen with your heart.* Think: "I want God's best for you. People deserve to be loved. I am going to show my love to you by listening."

4. *Listen with your mind.* Ask yourself: *What is this person trying to say to me? Is the information accurate? What need is she meeting through this conversation? Are there hidden messages? Can I 'read between the lines' to receive the real message?* Words can often mask the real message.

A child asks a new neighbor, "Do you have a dog?" He may be asking out of his love for dogs or out of his fear for dogs.

5. *Listen objectively.* Consciously tune out your needs and remove any biases which could block the message.

6. *Avoid distractions and interruptions.* Doodling or writing while another talks disconnects eye contact and focuses attention away from the person's need.

If a phone rings, you may choose not to answer it. Who deserves your time: the one who has made the effort to be in your presence, or the one who calls by phone? (If you have ever been in a department store trying to get waited on and the salesperson takes a telephone call instead of assisting you, you understand how the other person feels in this situation.)

7. *Stay tuned in.* Listening is an active process. Encourage a person to talk with your facial expression, a nod, or an occasional "uh—huh" just to let him know you are still listening. Or you may say, "Tell me more about . . ." In conversational listening, to encourage people to talk, ask questions about them and their families. Wait for a suspended pause before entering the conversation. To let a person know you have listened and to let him know if you have heard correctly, say back to him what he has said. This is called *feedback* or *reflection*— letting the other person *hear* what he *said* just as he would look into a mirror to see himself. A spouse, a friend, or a child feels appreciated when you can put into words what he has said. You might say, "I hear you saying that . . ." "So, what you are saying is . . ."

A child comes home from school totally disgusted with what happened that day. The teacher was mean and unreasonable. The mother listens and reflects: "So you had a hard time at school today. You're just feeling really unhappy about it all."

The child will say yes if that is an accurate reflection, or he will correct what you have said if you did not hear correctly.

A child, a spouse, or a friend feels so good when you listen and reflect and do not judge or try to jack him up. A person feels that someone, just someone, understands him. Then that person is more free to handle his feelings and to move on to more productive things.

When you give feedback, do it in a relaxed, unhurried manner—you are not parroting information—you are letting the other person know you did, indeed, listen.

8. *Listen from the other person's point of view.* Preschoolers (and children up to ages six or seven) do not think like adults. You will misjudge a child if you do not understand her thinking. A self-centered child (one who is able to think only from her view) is not intentionally trying to make you angry when she comes running inside with a newly discovered worm at a time when you are resting in bed. She only knows how much she wants to share her discovery with a favorite person. You can encourage her awe and wonder instead of scolding her.

Listen to a four-year-old's grand imagination which sounds like outright lying to you—unless you know that at this age what he thinks in his head is as real as if it happened.

A man lashed out at his fellow workers placing blame on them for not doing what he thought they should do. One person took the man to lunch and listened. He shared a story of fear, sorrow, and anxiety. He had been placed in a new job with an unreasonable work load, his wife was dying of cancer, and in his hurt he cried for help. One could no longer be angry knowing the difficult situation. An attitude of "how can I best help you during this trying time" brought comfort and relief.

When you listen from another's point of view, you are dignifying or valuing the other person. People talk about what is important to them. It may not be important to you, unless you choose to make it so. People talk about their fears, hopes, dreams, anxieties, and problems—those things they are not handling well.

Listening is two-way communication. It requires a sender and a receiver. In the case of listening, it may be more blessed to receive than to give. The one who receives may be giving the most.

9. *Learn to stay tuned in to the person talking, but think ahead.* Where is this leading? What is the speaker getting at? Don't jump to conclusions, just consider the possibilities.

10. *Try to reconstruct what was said when the conversation concludes.*

11. *When you listen, you do not have to agree or disagree, take sides, judge the goodness or badness, or the rightness or wrongness.* You can accept the reality of the person speaking and communicate "I hear you."

A boxing trainer and exchamp adopted a child who had lived in poverty and who often stole for food. This child was caught stealing something and was deeply sorry that he had done something to hurt his new dad. His adoptive father said: "Son, when I was you age, I stole something, too. I know that you will never do it again." Years later when the young man was asked, "Did you ever do it again?" he replied, "I never did."

A tearful woman in her fifties shared with me her inability to cope with a recently widowed brother-in-law who traveled many miles and came unannounced to her door. He simply could not handle his wife's death. She said, "I'm no psychiatrist, and he needs help."

People having difficulty coping with the loss of a loved one or problems at work or home sometimes desperately need someone to talk to who will LISTEN. They do not need sympathy or pity. They need someone to show enough love to just listen.

Listening to another makes a statement about yourself. If you love yourself, you can forget yourself and turn your thoughts toward another.

12. *In business or conversational listening, when you feel the need to disagree or to offer another opinion, first consider the consequences.* You take a risk when you give an opinion in opposition to the opinion of one in authority over you. If you choose to proceed, knowing the risk, consider couching your disagreement in words which begin with some agreement with the other person's view. "I can see your point on

that. I was wondering, however, if you had considered . . ." Agree with others whenever you can. State your positions positively but in such a way as to get a hearing.

People listen from their own experiences, their own needs, and security or insecurity. They frequently hear what they want to hear and not what another is trying to communicate.

Let's suppose that you are called by your manager: "Please come to my office immediately." Do you suddenly panic inside? *What have I done now?* you think. Do you expect the worst or do you wonder: *Am I getting the award for best employee this week?*

Or you may say to yourself, *I will go and be open to the experience. I am unafraid. I happily go to see what the need is.* Once you catch on to the art of active, attentive listening, you feel free to be who you are. You gain such freedom in relating (talking) with yourself and others. A basic honesty invades you and owns you.

YOUR TURN: Find a partner with whom you can work. Tell your partner how you feel about yourself. Mention how you felt as a child and how you feel now. Then listen as that person feeds back what you said. Then you listen as the other shares, and you give the feedback. If you do not have a partner for this kind of practice, try your skills during your next conversation. When you are alone, evaluate how well you did. Rate yourself on the 12 guidelines stated on the previous pages. On a sheet of paper or in your notebook, write the numbers 1 to 12 down the side. By each number, write a sentence describing what you did well. Happy listening to yourself and others!

9

LOVE LIFE: SAVOR THE MOMENT

"Whatever your hand finds to do, verily, do it with all your might" (Eccl. 9:10).

When my husband was miraculously returned to normalcy after over two years of medical depression, he would awaken early (4:30 a.m.), spring out of bed, and sing in his own inimitable (he has never been known for singing) way, "This is the day the Lord hath made, let us rejoice and be glad." Preferring to remain the night person that I am even after eleven years of arriving at work at or about seven, I was jolted by his early morning music. Negative thoughts bombarded me, *This is disgusting. Doesn't he know that I need my sleep?* My positive thoughts quickly came to my defense: *Oh, God, I will rejoice and be glad. This man who was dead to life is now alive. Let me rejoice with him.* Since his recovery, now over a year, he still works late into the night and arises early in the morning as if he is redeeming the time he lost. Whereas he was overcome with sadness, no motivation to work, loss of appetite, sleep disturbances, distorted thinking (which he was aware of but powerless to change), he is now savoring every moment. His days are spent showing compassion for others—that includes me.

Saturday has been our fun day only for the past year. Most of our married life I have either worked at the church or taught school. Thus, Saturday was our workday to prepare for Sunday. We prepared clothes, cooked the Sunday dinner (usually we had guests—whomever we or the children chose to invite home with us from church), and prepared to teach Sunday School. We cleaned house on Saturdays because the parsonage for about fifteen years was used for Sunday School rooms.

On our last two Saturday *fun* days, my husband has said: "Would you go with me to the hospital for just a moment? I want to see Jimmy

Randolph. You know he has been disabled a long time. And, also, Mr. Kennedy's sister died. I want to stop by the funeral home and be with him."

Just this last Saturday as we drove away from the city toward a shopping mall, I noticed Fred driving in a different direction from the place we had planned to go. He needed to take some fresh turnip greens by to Mike—a gunshot victim just out of the hospital and confined to bed. Mike enjoyed the last ones he took so much.

Every moment is a jewel to be received—a sparkling diamond, a priceless moment which is yours for the taking. Savor it. "This is the day the Lord hath made!"

"One today is worth two tomorrows. What I am to be I am now becoming," said the wise Benjamin Franklin. So how will I choose to use my day? And I want to follow wisely the words, "Choose for yourselves today whom you will serve" (Josh. 24:15).

A MOMENT WASTED IS A MOMENT LOST

How do you play the waiting game? The waiting that occurs at a traffic light, in line at the grocery store, while on hold on the telephone, when the computer is sluggish or down, when a credit card is being cleared? Moments such as these compose a part of our brief span of life on this planet.

A MOMENT WISELY USED IS A MOMENT GAINED

Pile up the moments. I recently received a birthday card congratulating me for being in the high numbers now. I was informed that I am 1,893,456,000 seconds old. (I'm older than I thought.) But then it reminds me that "It is easier to remember 39." It is so wonderful being 39 again and again and again.

Making the most, redeeming the time—is this your choice?

On a long trip from Louisiana to Kentucky, I recall driving through a town in which streets were under construction. Already experiencing several delays, I stopped for the traffic light and decided to rest my eyes. Fortunately, my adolescent son was at my side to awaken me shortly after the light turned green. At other times I choose to enjoy rather than be annoyed by what could be an outright inconvenience.

Many plans have been conceived and many minivacations experienced while standing in line. Closing my eyes briefly I can be transported in my mind's eye to a sunny beach in Hawaii. The sight and sounds of peaking waves of water are vivid in my mind.

We now know that what we see in our mind's eye is as real to us as what we see with our eyes. Both send electrical impulses that reach the vision center of the brain. This is as true of four-year-olds as it it for adults. Four-year-olds are often accused of lying because they tell you what they see in their mind's eye. They cannot distinguish the difference between what they imagine, or dream, and what they see with their eyes. How wonderful the gift of imagination! How magnificent the speed of thoughts. Thoughts can move forward or backward in time. We are fearfully and wonderfully made! (Ps. 139:14). Our bodies cannot a prison make. My body may be stationary while waiting, but my spirit (my intellect, emotion, and will) is free to travel. The spirit which dwells within is not confined to time or space.

When the weather permits, my husband and I do our daily walk in the area where we live. We climb on a hill where the road stops, and the top of the hill looms ahead. Yesterday, I felt challenged to leave the road's end and pursue the mountain. My only reluctance was: Could I walk briskly up the mountainside through the woods and maintain the speed necessary to maximize the effectiveness of my walk? My husband reminded me that we would probably exert more effort climbing the hill than we would walking briskly on flat ground. I accepted the challenge to discover new territory, to forge ahead. Paradoxically, when you exert or expend energy, you get energy. When you savor the moment of expended effort, you gain the moment of ecstasy. Sometimes the strain on muscles and the tilted slant of the body proceeding uphill brings a momentary weariness and struggle. While I am one who advocates looking up and onward, I find that when I look down, the road appears level and not steep. I do not think of the difficulty of the climb ahead, but the conquering of the road that lies immediately under my feet. My mind communicates to my legs, *Give a push of energy, exert a little more effort, and walk with a little more speed.* Before I know it, I have climbed the mountain. Headed toward my high goal, I accomplish it with each step I take and each moment I use. Just as a journey of a thousand miles begins with the first step, the journey of a lifetime is consumed moment by moment. Someone has said that today is the first day of the rest of your life. Another says, "Live as if this were the last day of your life." I say, "Live as if it is the first and the last day. Live as if it is the first by forgetting what is past and pressing on toward what is ahead. Live as if it is your last by doing what is important and eternal now. A young man with terminal cancer celebrates each moment of life. He has accepted his circumstances and is using it to the fullest. He thinks and breathes and behaves in keeping with an eternal perspective. He rejoices with the opportunity each moment brings.

SAVOR THE STAGE OF LIFE

Give to a child his childhood, lest he have to delay it until a time when it is difficult on the person and his loved ones. David Elkind, author of the books *The Hurried Child* and *Miseducation*, exposes the ill effects of denying a child his childhood. The hurried child, the one made to behave and think like an adult, has the usual stress symptoms: headaches and stomachaches in preschoolers, learning problems, and depression in elementary school children. Miseducation, pressuring the children academically to become superkids, has more deep-seated and long-term effects, sometimes leaving the children emotionally disabled for a lifetime.

One woman said, "I am living with a 38-year-old child. His parents went the route of pushing the academics—making him a superkid. He never had his childhood, but he is having it now. He is doing all those things he was not allowed to do as a child."

Childhood is a special season designed by God. The dependent, literal-minded, illogical child does not think like adults. But what he thinks makes sense to him. If children were really logical, how would we ever convince them of the tooth fairy, flying reindeer, one Santa Claus for the whole world delivering gifts to each child on a single evening? Let us reverence the special years when the child is most impressionable, when he is forming his self-image, when adults can make no mistakes, and when adults have the authority over the child. If you are a parent of young children or you teach or have contact with them, remember this sobering thought, Young children think God is most like the important people in their lives. This calls for us to be the best possible models or examples of godly living—savoring each moment, living it fully. The legacy of living life to the fullest each moment of the day can be passed on to our children. And *we* can learn from the children. A book entitled *The Ministry of the Child* by Dennis C. Benson and Stan J. Stewart crossed my desk. Hurriedly I read the title and wondered if an error had been made. The only books I had seen on a similar subject were about the ministry *to* children. With a little reflection on the subject, I arrived at the conclusion: Yes, children do indeed minister to us. In the first place, children live in the here and now—just what this chapter on savoring the moment is inviting you to do. The here and now is all we have now. Children do not dwell on the past, nor do they concern themselves with the future.

Traveling home on a narrow, winding road one night, a young serviceman home on leave for a wedding was tragically killed in an automobile accident. While visiting in the home of his grieving parents, I suddenly became aware of the ministry of a newborn baby, God's gift to the young man's sister. I was reminded that when Jesus was faced with death, He always spoke of life. In the midst of those grieving over the death of one so young and vibrant was the innocent face of a newborn baby bringing solace and hope to saddened hearts. When I look into the eyes of a child, I am enriched for the moment with the handiwork of God—God's love note. "I have sent you something to love and to cherish which, in turn, will love you."

No matter what age we are, we seldom think that death is really for us. We are constantly reminded by the media of those who have died. If questioned, we will admit that death is inevitable, but we dismiss thoughts that it will happen to us. We are going to die, but between birth and death is a marvelous span of life. Because the span is as a twinkling of the eye in many respects, I want to seize every moment as blessed and hallowed.

Each stage of life brings with it unique opportunities for joys and sorrows, fulfillment and crises. The crises most common to specific stages call for readjustments in life. Youth are searching for their niche in life—making choices about careers and marriage (to marry or not to marry). Young adults cope with establishing a home and providing for a family. Middle adults struggle with providing for their own children who are entering college and the work force. They feel the emotions of "the empty nest." Older adults cope with aging parents and what is happening in the lives of their adult children. No matter what age, each person is going through some crisis. Each person needs someone for emotional support. Support groups—people experiencing similar problems—can be a source of comfort and encouragement. You can be encouraged, and you can give encouragement. You can savor even the difficult experiences which allow you to give or receive love and care.

Look Back

The strains of the familiar "Climb Every Mountain" bring an exhilaration to my spirit. Climbing life's mountain is accompanied by music from above. Where I walk each day, I notice many walkers who are fortified with earphones piping music to their brains. They say they need it to keep up their pace and to make the time pass swiftly. I choose not to make my time pass swiftly—every moment is precious. I choose to savor the moments—never do I want to lose these moments hurriedly to get to the next—that's like eating a meal in haste so that you can get to the good part—the dessert. The meal—every bite—is to be enjoyed including the dessert. You can choose to relish all the courses which life dishes out. You can choose to make otherwise tedious work a thing to be coveted. A young woman playing the "martyr game"—my life is always worse than anyone's—complained that she had to work on her day off. I know many who would have traded their work for hers. You can make difficult work a joy. It is a matter of attitude. When you have hard work to do—tackle it first and say to yourself: *This is going to be fun. I choose to make it fun.* And with a song in your heart, you will have finished before you know it. The most decisive part is choosing to get started. Nothing is ever so difficult as taking the first step.

How many people are always chasing rainbows, never aware of the rainbows which surround them—always waiting for the best, not knowing the best is now?

As I near the top of my mountain, I pause to look back. I can enjoy the memories of childhood, youth, young, and middle adulthood without having to live in the past. My memories are a wellspring of resources upon which I draw for nourishment and thirst quenching. We have so many treasures and resources within from which we can learn. Jesus was asking us to use these memories when He told us to "do to others what we would have done unto us." You have to think about what has happened to you that brought you joy or pain. Those things that brought you joy would probably bring others joy. You learn to do those things for others. Those things that caused you pain—words and action—you learn not to do to others. We have to get in touch with our own experiences and discover on the basis of what we know, how we will treat others. We also are called upon to think from the other person's point of view to know what he would appreciate. What a wonderful world it would be if you and I treated everyone else the way we prefer to treated!

Look back to your roots. They can give you "self" insight. Your self-esteem is largely developed by age four or five, the result of how you saw yourself in the mirror of the important people in you life. The child of your inner past lives on within you. Are you still very much the kind of person you were as a child? Do you like what you discover when you think of your childhood—your fears, your favorite things, the joys, the way your parents treated you, the important people in your life?

When I look back, these are the images I retrieve:

Fears.— My father was in college preparing for the ministry during my early years. In the biology lab was a huge glass jar with the dissected head of a man.

Across the street was a man who had a phonograph which at one time fascinated me. The steel cup for holding the phonograph needles was missing, exposing a dark hole beneath. This neighbor who was missing one finger told me that he lost it when he put his finger in that hole.

Until recently I would not wear the color lavender, became nauseated at the fragrance of carnations and gardenias, and abhorred the sight of textured gray velveteen (popular for a season for women's coats). Each of these which I avoided was associated with funerals I experienced as a child. Shrouds were mostly lavender, Cape Jasmin (the domestic variety of gardenia) and carnations were among the most fragrant of the floral arrangements, and caskets were covered with gray textured velveteen. Until I reached into my past and faced the source of my anxious feelings, I could not get rid of them. I now court opportunities to wear lavender and smell gardenias. I have yet to discover that gray textured velveteen is an appropriate material for ladies' coats.

Moments of delight.—In the two-story white dormitory house where my family lived, I remember the bathroom at the end of a long side porch—bathtime in a white bathtub with my mother was quality time. When I was in graduate school, I was consumed with being both a graduate assistant and a student. My nights were spent writing papers. Using the rewards which were available to me at that particular time, I would say, "Sybil, when you have worked for two hours on the paper, you may take a nice, warm bath." You can savor moment after moment in a 20-minute minivacation in the bathtub. (That computes to 1200 moments recorded in seconds.) Receiving the sensations of warm, bubbly water, I can close my eyes and hear the strains of tropical music coming from the beach. Such luxury! The commonplace can become uncommon and re-create the spirit. The child of my inner past comes out to play when I make of bathing in the bathtub the same quality of recreation as bathing in the sun.

Lying on my back in the grass looking up at the blue sky laced with white clouds was a favorite *pasttime*. (No, it was not to "pass time" but to savor it.) As the clouds changed into different shapes and forms, I would decide what the images looked like—continuous transformations of monsters, giants, animals large and small, flowers, trees—all these and many more appeared and faded in my sight. And today I lie outside captivated by the "pictures" the clouds make, and I relish anew my childish wonders.

The sight of violets translates me to my childhood when a walk in the green pasture near the stream always yielded many delights—the tickling of soft, resilient grass under my feet and the sight and satiny feel of violets dotted among the grass-blades. More beautiful than orchids to me is their tiny delicate resemblance.

Get in touch with your childhood to rediscover the awe and wonder of God's magnificent creation. Everything is so new and just waiting to be discovered. The world of creation comes to a marvelous crescendo in autumn. This autumn has produced the most vivid and breathtaking colors of my entire lifetime (and that is a long time). Autumn must be God's favorite season. Surrounded by hills I notice that God has the trees cloaked in a coat of many colors. As I sit at my dining room table where I write, my view of the scalloped hills reveals matchless color bursts ranging in hue from luscious golden iridescent yellow to incandescent reds and glowing browns. My soul sings new words to a familiar song, "The hills are alive with their autumn colors, glowing afresh with His *matchless* love."

How refreshing to experience the "burning bush(es)"! Elizabeth Barrett Browning has said it this way:

> "Earth's crammed with heaven,
> And every common bush afire with God;
> But only he who sees, takes off his shoes—
> The rest sit round it and pluck blackberries."

YOUR TURN: Close your eyes and reminisce. Go back as far as you can remember . . . five, four, three? Think of the things which brought you pleasure. Write these down. Discover your childish fears which may still encumber you. Deal with these. Make a commitment to letting the child within you come out to play. List those things which you can still enjoy and will choose to enjoy to reenergize you.

When I look back to where I came from and latch onto the memories, I am reminded of God's plan for me. In childhood He set me apart. He ordained me for a special mission in life. I knew it then and even more so now. He has a special plan for you, too. Continue discovering how God can best use you. When I was a child my father was a minister. He was then, and remained until his death, a very conservative minister of the gospel. My father and my mother gave me both roots and wings. I value and savor my legacy. I wish for all children loving, caring parents who are Christlike.

"GIMME A BREAK"

When you savor the moment, you live life with gusto. You work when you work, and you play when you play. When you do not take time to play, you reduce your productivity. When you play, you can go back to your work with a greater freedom and motivation. You can accomplish more faster and better. Why else would we have "breaks" where we work?

Never talk "work" on your break. Did I say *never*? Never say *never*. The purpose of *break* is to "break from your work." Take breaks and spice them with variety—different people, places, *beverages*, snacks, activities. Amazingly enough, you can have a wonderful break without food (I *never* thought I would say that). You may use a break to listen to music, read a book, write a note, make a telephone call, plan something exciting. Make a list of things from which to choose.

YOUR TURN: Make a list. Some new ideas I have for breaks are:

Take control of your breaks—and savor every wonderful moment.

ACCEPT THE REALITIES OF LIFE

Death is a very real part of life. We hurt when we are separated from loved ones. We can, however, savor God's comfort and the loving touch of friends.

When my father died, God worked a miracle in me. Years before when my father had a heart attack, the doctor advised me not to return home which was several states away. I was overcome with fear at the thought of losing my father. At night I would lie in bed at my mother's house and shake uncontrollably. Also, I was fearful that I would abort my unborn child if I did not get control of myself. My father lived long enough to see his granddaughter born and to be comforted by his granddaughter's two-year-old son when he went to the hospital for his last time.

During my father's last week on earth, I was privileged to stay overnight with him in the hospital and hear his soul's sincere desire expressed, "I am ready to go home, Sybil, and I don't mean my home in Minden, I mean my heavenly home." Knowing his suffering and the misery of gasping for every breath, I lovingly commended his soul to

God. Although I believe a daughter could not love a father more, I did not weep at his funeral, nor have I wept since. My father left me a legacy of love and joy and reconciliation. I cherish every memory. I praise my God for being so richly blessed through a righteous father.

One of the greatest tributes to my father came recently when my daughter's father-in-law said to her seven-year-old son, McIntyre, who had just done a tender, compassionate deed, "You are just like your Daddy Paul (my father)."

Savoring the moment is knowing that God has placed you where you are and has been preparing you throughout your lifetime for this very hour. And, you are not anxious about the future, merely open to God's will and work in your life. The mystery is not knowing what God has in store for tomorrow, but you know the all-knowing, all-loving God is working out the purpose He has for you.

To be consciously aware of God working with and through you is to *savor the moment*.

YOUR TURN: Write down some painful experiences through which you received the comfort of God and of friends who cared.

Now think of a recent time when you have been able to comfort another.

Who do you know who needs your encouragement—who needs to know that somebody really cares?

Decide what you can and will do to touch this life.

10

STOP NONPRODUCTIVE BEHAVIOR

"Do all things without grumbling or disputing" (Phil. 2:14).

I wish I knew who to give credit to for the cartoon which showed only the head of a woman (it could have easily been a man) in each of the first three pictures. Above each head was captioned, "So far today I haven't criticized or found fault." "I haven't spread gossip—I've tried to see only good." "I've been patient and kind—my thoughts loving and caring." The last picture shows a woman getting out of bed saying, "But now that it's time to get up, Lord, I'll need all the help I can get."

A young minister preaching to a group of senior citizens graphically described heaven and hell and queried, "How could anyone make the wrong choice?" My thought focused on the present moment, and my silent question was, "Why would anyone choose misery over happiness any day of this earthly life?"

You choose to be happy or miserable. If you choose to be happy and productive, you will want to take inventory and determine if you are weighted down with these self-defeating behaviors: complaining, blaming, worrying, criticizing, whining, feeling sorry for yourself, mishandling anger.

You want to learn how to live life more fully, or you would not have read this book. So, if you want to savor the moment—every moment, you can choose to stop the nonproductive, time-wasting, energy-depleting, debilitating behaviors which rob you of your joy.

COMPLAINING

"You would complain if you were hung with new rope," a husband said to his wife. And she probably could have said the same about him.

Could this be said of you? I overheard two people complaining about their problems at work. When asked if they worked in the area about which they complained, they responded no. The question which I kept to myself was, "Then why do you spend your valuable once-in-a-lifetime moment complaining about something for which you are not accountable and over which you have no control?" Complaining may be a stop-gap measure you take to avoid doing something about a problem.

Time is the substance of which life is made. Think of time as an investment. How you use it determines the dividends you will receive. When you use it wisely, touching lives in such a way as to encourage (infuse courage) and comfort, the dividends are compounded daily. When you work diligently toward accomplishing your purposes, the payoff is immediate in the joy and satisfaction which you feel.

So to rid yourself of the cumbersome, nonessential, useless baggage you are carrying, program your mind to think productive-inspiring thoughts. Say over and over to yourself, "I choose not to complain."

OUT OF THE HEART ARE THE ISSUES OF LIFE (PROV. 4:23, KJV).

YOUR TURN: Be honest and check what you believe to be the reason for your complaints. When you get your feelings out in the open so you can look at them, then you can more easily choose to change what you do not like—those feelings which are holding you back.

Complaints arise from the heart of one who feels:

    insecure (complaining is something to hide behind—to keep the
           spotlight off of me),

    dumped upon (I have to do someone else's work),

    imposed upon (I have to do what you should be doing),

    unappreciated,

    criticized more than affirmed,

    treated unfairly (have to do more work than others),

    expected to do more than I can do,

    pressured beyond my ability to cope,

    taken in (caught holding the bag),

    no one cares about me and my feelings,

    lack of affirmation (I never hear from him unless he wants

something),

nothing is ever quite right (the food is horrible, the bed is too
soft/too hard, the temperature is too hot/too cold),

inferior—not enough (this often comes across as a feeling of supe-
riority—"I wish she would buy another dress. I am so
tired of looking at that one." "I wish she would cut her
hair. It would be so much more becoming." "Just look
at the colors he is wearing."),

everything must be perfect (cannot tolerate others' human
imperfections).

What a burden to feel the need to make others the way you want
them. What arrogance! If you checked any on the previous list, please
know that you can be relieved of these burdensome weights which you
are carrying. In your mind's eye, slowly lower your burdens to the
ground and say to yourself, "I choose to remove the chip (or the logs)
from my shoulders. Too long I have born an unnecessary burden. I
choose to use my energy productively. I will replace my burdensome
bag of complaints with the buoying words of self-affirmation. I will
major on my strengths and practice to overcome my weakness. I will
be accountable *for* me and *to* me for my own behavior and my own
work."

YOUR TURN: Preview your day thus far. Write down any complaints which you made. Look at each one and ask, "Can I do anything
to solve the problem?" Choose either to write your plans to solve the
problems or write this statement, "I choose not to complain."

BLAMING: EXCUSES EXCUSES

Blaming is a cop-out. It means making someone or something other
than yourself responsible for your situation and behavior—not accepting responsibility for you own actions and words.

Young children are often accused of blaming their "misbehavior" on
something or somebody. Remember, however, they do not think like
adults—they are limited in experience with which to think—they are
illogical. The child touches a vase which falls to the floor and breaks.
You may inappropriately accuse the child of lying when the child says
no in answer to your question, "Did you do that?" (Avoid asking a

question when you already know the answer.) In the mind of a child who does not yet know cause and effect, he did not do it. He was not even touching it when it broke; the floor must have done it. It broke when it hit the floor. Parents will do well to explain situations over and over until the child learns what the cause is and what the effect is. "You picked up the vase; the vase dropped to the floor and broke." Why should a toddler or two-year-old (who does not know the value of a vase) be held responsible?

YOUR TURN: What blame statements have you made today?

Mentally, put a check by these or similar statements which you made.

> The cake fell. The weather wasn't right. Something was wrong with the oven.
>
> I am late because it rained (snowed); the alarm didn't go off.
>
> I just didn't have time to do it.
>
> If he hadn't pulled out in front of me, I wouldn't have hit him.
>
> I wanted to get to church (or some other place) on time, but my husband (wife, child, the driver) delayed me.
>
> I would play golf (have a hobby), too, if I had as much money or time on my hands as he does.
>
> I could have a dream house, too, if I had the money they have.
>
> I could get my work in on time, too, if I had the secretarial help he has.
>
> I could get organized, too, if I didn't have anymore to do than she has.
>
> I could feel better about my work, too, if I took off as much as she does.

You may want to read this aloud to yourself. "I am an adult. I am able and capable. I am valuable and worthwhile. God made me one of a kind with a special mission to fulfill. I will accept responsibility for my own behavior. Nobody else but me is responsible for what I do— not my mother, my father, my boss, any other employee, my family members, my friends, or any other person. I will not blame my circumstances—my childhood, my birth order (middle child, first child, only child) and on and on. What I do, I do of my own free will. I choose to take responsibility for my own actions. I will not place blame on anyone or on my circumstances. From henceforth, I will accept blame for the choices I make."

People find it so difficult to accept blame when the truth is that once you are able to, you feel such a freedom. You find yourself saying, "I will take responsibility for that." "I accept the blame." "That was my fault."

YOUR TURN: Now look at the preceding blame statements and rewrite those you checked taking responsibility for your action. For example: "I just didn't have time to do it" might be changed to "I chose to spend my time doing something else."

WORRYING

When our third child Mark was an adolescent, he heard a minister preach on the subject of *worrying*—"Fret not yourself." Notice in Psalm 37, three times these same words appear. Worrying has been and is a behavior common to human beings. So impressed with the minister's distinction between worry and concern, Mark would constantly remind me, "Don't worry, Mom, just be concerned." When I find myself worrying, Mark's words, emblazoned in my memory, remind me to choose to be concerned rather than to worry.

The summer before Mark finished college, he made a dream come true. Knowing that such an opportunity might never come again, he planned a bike trip which began at Berea, Kentucky, and ended in Pueblo, Colorado. His father and I watched him load the car with bike, tent, stove, dried food, map, and writing supplies—all except the bike carefully weighed and contained in nylon bags which he had made. As we gave him our farewell hugs and best wishes before he drove to Kentucky, Mark noted the taut look on my face and responded, "Mother, don't worry, just be concerned." For over six weeks Mark was on the bike trail alone (none of his friends could make the trip at that time). Not knowing exactly where he was, knowing the hilly terrain, and the prevalence of tornadic conditions (I remembered that Dorothy in the Wizard of Oz lived in Kansas through which he would pass), knowing that he was accepting the hospitality of strangers (some on the trail invited him in for the night), knowing his vulnerability to theft—my concern mounted as the weeks stretched on.

When he set up tent at night, he could not leave it unattended. A mother who worries can imagine the worst. What does worrying help? Nothing. What does worrying hurt? You.

I have wasted too much time worrying and mostly about things that never happened. As I was writing this chapter and renewing my own commitment not to worry but to be concerned instead, I was faced with the following test. I had taken a vacation day to work at home on writing assignments. My husband and I had planned to leave later in the day to drive to Richmond, Kentucky, for the Eastern Kentucky University homecoming game, our first since leaving there 11 years ago. That morning my husband said, "I will see you at noon." I responded: "Now don't rush me. I have a deadline to meet. I may not be finished by noon." He did not show up at noon. At three o'clock, he had not returned. I began to worry: *Fret not yourself, Mom; don't worry, be concerned.* This was unlike Fred. I expressed my concern by calling the traffic bureau (no accident in the vicinity in which he was expected to travel had been reported—I might call the hospitals). Following the advice given by the traffic bureau, I called the hospitals in the vicinity of his route. My concern was relieved when the results were negative—no accident—no admittance of a person by that name. When Fred returned shortly after three o'clock, he was surprised that he could cause such concern. He thought he was honoring my request, "Don't rush me!"

You may worry about one of the following: the health and safety of you and your loved ones, the threat of natural disasters or war, financial security, work problems, getting along with people, possibility of failure, being embarrassed or rejected, and on and on. Mostly, worries are unfounded or needless. Most situations have happy endings. Some situations do have unhappy endings; but even if your worst fears came to pass, would your worrying have helped? When worst comes to worst, we can receive His comfort. His grace *is* sufficient.

YOUR TURN: Think of the last three situations which caused you to worry. Write these on a sheet of paper. Beside each write the outcome of the situation.

How would you have behaved differently if you had chosen, instead of worrying, to be concerned?

The title of a popular song "Don't Worry. Be Happy" is imprinted in many shapes, sizes, and forms on sweat-shirts and T-shirts for young and old. The song reminds us that all people have some trouble—and when you worry, the trouble is double.

CRITICIZING?

Why do people criticize others? Criticism is one way to focus attention away from self to another person. It is like hiding behind someone. Someone once said to me, "You cannot hide behind someone unless you are smaller than they are."

You are really trying to say: "I'm better than that. I don't make those mistakes." Or, "Hey, look at me. I would never be guilty of that." Actually, though, what we criticize in others may be like seeing our own inadequacies in the mirror of others. Now, when I find myself even thinking a critical thought of another, I ask myself: "Why is this bothering me? What in me is this behavior touching off?" I may be saying unconsciously, "I don't like this behavior in me, and I dislike this even more when I see it in someone else." When I criticize, I have an opportunity to learn more about me than the other person.

Do you enjoy being criticized? What do you really want to hear others say about you? Had you rather that others notice your strengths or your weaknesses? One of my college professors frequently used this statement, "Nothing succeeds like success, and nothing fails like failure."

Both children and adults thrive on being noticed when they do something appropriate and withdraw when someone mostly notices their mistakes. The natural consequences of our mistakes is punishment enough. We know when we fail, and to have someone tell us is to put salt in our open wounds.

As a supervisor of student teachers at the university, I urged teachers to notice, notice, notice what a child did when it even approached being appropriate behavior. One morning I observed while a student teacher taught a kindergarten class. I recorded 25 tally marks—one for each time I heard Charles's name called when he was being reprimanded. When we had our conference following the three-hour session, I mentioned that she had called Charles's name 25 times for doing something "wrong." "I wonder what Charles is learning about himself?" I asked.

Charles is learning that he is a "bad" boy. He is learning to get attention in the way he best knows how. I suggested, "Suppose you call Charles's name 25 times during the next three-hour session for things he does that are appropriate such as finishing what he starts, helping another, walking instead of running, or returning a puzzle to the rack. Thank him for every attempt to behave in a productive manner. Then watch him change day-by-day from a caterpillar into a butterfly."

CONDEMNING

Those who feel most faulty find themselves finding fault—putting down another. "Have you noticed that he always leaves early and today he was 15 minutes late?" "I wish she would write legibly. I don't know how she expects me to read her writing." "He wastes more time." "Her desk is so cluttered. I don't know how she finds anything." "He surely is getting fat." "I wish she would keep her lawn mowed and her hedge cut. What a mess!" "He's just plain stingy." "She is so self-righteous!"

Fault-finding statements—all of these. When all of the condemning is said and done, who is helped? Who is hurt? Who is hurt most? People are for loving and encouraging. People are not for putting down—and that includes you, too.

Replace every thought which condemns or puts down with a thought that affirms and uplifts. Start affirming yourself. Each day talk to yourself about your accomplishments. Notice your own work and contributions. When others compliment you, accept the compliment. Some people have a difficult time accepting compliments. When you hear, "What a beautiful dress you are wearing!" you may say: "It is really too short. I need to let the hem out." Or, "You did a great job of organizing your garage!" and you say, "It's still really in a mess—someday I will get it right." For two reasons, don't put yourself down. You will feel better yourself and when you feel fully affirmed, you will have less need to condemn others. Be your own best friend. Do to yourself what you wish others would do to you. Also, when you do not accept the compliment, you are putting down the one who made it.

Among the many people I know, I find few who consciously strive to affirm and not condemn. And you can always find something positive and worthwhile to say. I know one man about whom it is said, "I've never heard him say anything bad about anyone." Neither have I heard him complain or place blame. He is a happy man!

WHINING?

Whining is a childish form of complaining. When you whine, you do not really care if another hears what you have to say. You just want someone to know you are unhappy about something in the hopes they will do what it is that will make you happy. Children whine about what they want and do not want. "I want something to drink" "I want you to hold me." "I want to watch TV." "I don't want to go to bed." "I don't want to pick up my toys." When a child's whining has been reinforced, the person grows up continuing to use the behavior which works. Are you one who whines to manipulate (work) people? What better way, more grown-up way, could you use to make your wishes known? Choose to express your wants in a reasonable and intelligible manner. Choose to be adult in your communication.

FEELING SORRY FOR YOURSELF

Had any pity parties lately? Have you felt so sorry for yourself that you just had a good cry? Why do we feel the need to feel sorry for ourselves? Have you known those people who seemed to thrive on "Woe-is-me" stories and statements? They have to tell about how difficult life is for them, how their spouses abuse them, how their operation was the worst anyone ever had, and how they are going to be sick for a long time. Life IS bad for them. They feel nobody loves them, comes to see them, or calls them. They are wrapped up and smothering in their own self-pity, blaming their unhappiness on sources outside themselves.

Self-pity dissolves when you give yourself to brightening the life of another. A dear friend, a victim of cancer and bleeding internally and externally lies in the intensive care ward of the hospital. But that does not keep her from remembering my birthday with a card. This saint will exit this world not thinking about herself but others. Cheerful, hopeful, feeling that she has everything to gain and nothing to lose, she is totally cleansed of self-pity. Where love is, self-pity cannot abide.

MISHANDLING ANGER?

Do you get explosively angry (uncontrollably so) or do you have trouble getting angry or expressing anger? In either case, the result is self-defeating. We can look to the past to discover some reasons why we are as we are, but it is nonproductive to place blame on our parents for our mishandling of anger.

I know that my father was my model for handling anger. He was peaceful and accommodating by nature, and few times did I ever see him express his anger explosively. As a young man, he reportedly possessed and demonstrated a fiery temper. While I patterned my father's example, I cannot blame him for my lack of ability to express anger appropriately. I can choose to learn how to handle my anger by expressing it in timely and appropriate ways.

On one of our Saturday fun days, my husband and I were enroute to our agreed upon place when he suddenly took a turn off the designated route. When I inquired why he was making this turn, he said, "I want to go by the hospital for a moment to see this young man who is critically ill."

This was my fun day. I work very hard, have little time to play. It is *our* day. I was not asked to change any plans. Thoughts raced through my mind. I was absolutely furious—enraged. And glad I was feeling this rare emotion for me. As one who desires to think before she speaks (I don't always manage to), I carefully couched my thoughts into what I hoped would be tactful but would express what I needed to say. "The next time you make such plans, I would like to know ahead of time, so I will have a choice of participating."

When we arrived in the hospital parking lot, I was totally silent, feeling the pain of rage—burning inside and totally miserable. I had time to think. I savored the moment (can you believe that?). I said to myself: *I am glad for this experience. It gives me an opportunity to practice what I preach about handling anger. I choose to let this experience work for good. While my husband visits, I will use this time to get my walking in.* I donned my walking shoes which I keep in the car for opportunities that arise, and I *walked* and *walked*—with more briskness and energy than usual.

Actually the time involved was approximately 30 minutes—the time I needed for my daily walk. I had a choice of (1) exploding, (2) saying, "I felt enraged when you turned toward the hospital—I felt discounted, not considered," or (3) saying what I said. My purpose was to make a point without overdramatizing which has a tendency to boomerang. And I was able to say positive things to my husband, "I am so grateful that you care about people who are hurting." Most of the time my husband shows consideration for me beyond my expectations. I can choose joyfully to do some things with and for him which are as vitally important to him as my need for a fun day.

Paul wrote in Ephesians, "Be angry, and yet do not sin; do not let the sun go down on your anger" (4:26). Anger is healthy when directed toward the appropriate situations and events. We need to feel angry about injustices, poverty, abuses (physical, mental, emotional, sexual), drug problems, the exploitation of our environment, and man's inhumanity to man. Our anger toward such can best be expressed in an effort to stop that which causes abuse, pain, and suffering and does not respect the dignity of God's highest creation.

One mother who has lost a daughter because of an accident involving a drunken driver might respond with hate, bitterness, and vengeance. Another mother angry for the same cause expresses her anger by starting an organization called Mothers Against Drunk Drivers (MADD).

Anger unexpressed gnaws on the soul spreading like a malignancy. It affects the body's chemistry and causes physical problems such as ulcers, high blood pressure, heart problems, and mental and emotional problems (often diagnosed as depression). Sometimes you are unable to face the one with whom you are angry. When you cannot tell a person you are angry, you may feel better if you write how you feel—

this gets your anger outside yourself.

YOUR TURN: Write down how you felt the last time you were angry.

You can deal with your anger by expressing how you feel. "I feel angry when . . ." Your feelings will be better received when you say *how you feel* than when you accuse someone of making you angry as in "You make me so angry when . . ." Choose to handle your anger constructively. You want to express it in some way (written or spoken), and you want to be as redemptive as possible—wanting relief for yourself but not desiring to hurt another. This means no name calling, references to other situations, or physical abuse. Being upset is best conveyed when you are in control. Conclude a confrontation with positive words and touching (when you feel genuine and comfortable doing this).

Have you ever lost it with a fellow worker, a child, a spouse, a special friend, a classmate, your employer? A mother of two small children confided: "I blew it with my children today. They just whined, clung to me all day, didn't want to do anything productive—and all day they vied for my attention." You don't have to be perfect to be a good mother. Children can learn that sometimes Mother loses it, but mostly she remains calm no matter what. What you tell yourself is: *So what, I lost it. I will begin this moment in control, and I will live one moment at a time. I will say to myself, I choose not to get angry when my children beg and compete for my attention.* Accept the responsibility—don't blame the children by saying: "You make me so mad." You choose to get upset or angry. You can also choose the way you feel.

You can choose to feel angry or not feel angry. You can choose who or what you will allow to make you angry. You can choose to express anger in helpful ways or hurtful ways.

11

DEVELOP A POSITIVE ATTITUDE

"Have this attitude in yourselves which was also in Christ Jesus,. . . taking the form of a bond-servant, . . . He humbled himself" (Phil. 2:5,7-8).

You are able and capable. God made you that way. God gave you a free will—the freedom to choose, to make choices. What trust He placed in you and me! When you believe you have a choice of spiritual, mental, and emotional health, you will stop those self-defeating behaviors which injure and destroy your health.

Begin now to think, feel, and act as a person of worth and value knowing that God wants His best for you.

Take responsibility for what you think. When negative thoughts bombard or seem to sneak in, talk back to yourself. Instead of saying, "You make me so upset," say, "I choose to get upset when . . ."

Take responsibility for what you feel. "I choose to feel the way I feel. I feel happy (sad, glad, anxious, excited, overwhelmed, overcome) . . ." Tell yourself how you feel, and own your feelings—take responsibility for them. If they are debilitating, choose to change them.

ALWAYS BE JOYFUL

Grab opportunities to express optimism—a positive outlook. A professor tells the story of two young boys in the same family who were opposites—one was extremely pessimistic and the other, extremely optimistic. The parents wanted to encourage their pessimistic child and to cure the other child of his optimism. (Some people just can't stand optimism—they can't stand Pollyanna who changed the attitude of a community because of her positive thinking.) So the parents put under the Christmas tree a gleaming, red bicycle for the pessimistic child and a barrel of manure for the optimistic child. When the children came downstairs on Christmas morning to see what was under the tree, the pessimist saw the red bicycle and was disappointed because it was not blue. The optimist saw the barrel of manure and gleefully started looking for the pony.

A positive attitude, like adrenaline, releases energy. When you exert energy, you become energized. Doctors advise walking to relieve stress. Which comes first a positive attitude and walking or walking and a positive attitude? When you choose to put one foot forward, you are on your way.

What is the difference in two people given the same task? One person whose job is handling the work requests for the people in an office looks at you, smiles, and says thank you when you put a request in the box on the desk. Another person with the same job looks at you, does not smile, and says, "Not again."

Which person would you prefer to work with? Can you learn to respond happily and cheerfully when you are given tasks to do? Observe what happens when you are given a task and you smile and say thank you. Also notice what happens to you when you do the work cheerfully and unreluctantly and return the completed work on time. Then take a good look at your manager or employer as you genuinely inquire, "Is there anything else I can do for you?"

Fortunately, I am surrounded by people who seem to know what I need *before* I ask and respond in the positive manner I have described. I have learned from them.

A MATTER OF THE HEART

A positive attitude comes from within—from a heart filled with joy. Your outlook on life is not determined by circumstances. A grandmother, also the mother of two grown sons, was trying to convince herself that she had the right to leave her husband and marry a man who had a wife and family. Seeking someone to agree with her, she inquired, "Don't I deserve a little happiness?"

Happiness is not what you get from others, it is what you carry around with you—and it follows you wherever you go.

A positive attitude and happiness are complementary actions and reactions. They go together like love and marriage.

YOUR TURN: Finish these sentences:

My attitude is

To have the attitude of Christ, I will

HOORAH FOR LAUGHTER!

Two summers ago when my husband, Fred, was in major depression, we drove to Destin, Florida, for a week's vacation. Our apartment overlooked the Gulf. I was in desperate need for relaxation, rest, and a renewal of spirit. I took along several books to read. (The types of books you choose say much about your wants and needs.) My need was to get some control over my life, to think more positively, and gain courage and strength to continue in my current crisis. First, I read a book *Anatomy of an Illness* by Norman Cousins. Cousins tested the therapeutic potential of laughter. His return to health from a crippling spinal disease he attributes to self-prescribed daily doses of humor. Cousins likened laughing's physiological and psychological effects to that of jogging. Laughter is "internal jogging."

Psychiatrists have said that laughing a hundred times a day is equivalent to about ten minutes of rowing. A great deal of research is being done in this area. Laughter apparently stimulates the reproduction of alertness hormones called *catecholamines*. These hormones in turn trigger the release of endorphins. These create a sense of relaxation and well-being and dull the perception of pain. During laughter your heart rate, blood pressure, and muscular tension increase, and when laughter ceases, these levels drop below normal leaving one feeling relaxed. This relaxation can last 45 minutes after the last laugh and may be beneficial in reducing effects of heart disease, high blood pressure, and depression. Research is just now discovering to a greater extent what the writer of Proverbs knew so long ago, "A merry heart doeth good like a medicine" (Prov. 17:22, KJV).

YOUR TURN: What have you laughed about today? What will you do to get a good laugh?

CHEER UP!

You can have a merry heart.

1. *Surround yourself with wholesome things that bring cheer and laughter*—the Bible (book of joy), newspaper comic strips (funny ones), cartoons, videos, books, magazines, cards, audiotapes, posters, movies.

Look for humor in God's wonderful creation. When I peer into the face of a hippopotamus or watch a playful kitten or look up at a long-necked giraffe, I think, *How funny!* and silently chuckle. Choose those things which help you laugh.

One of my favorite ways to cheer myself is to look in the mirror and see myself without my false face (as I really am)—that's a laugh. After a few husky laughs, I feel great. I was affirmed recently when I read, "When you can laugh at yourself [and not just your face in the mirror], that is a sign of maturity."

I am reminded of the joke of the three little older ladies. One of them said: "You know, I am getting a little forgetful. When I find myself standing in front of the refrigerator with a bowl in my hand, I don't know whether I have just taken it out, or I am supposed to put it in."

To which another quickly responded: "Well, I haven't done that yet; but the other day, I found myself at the top on the stairs. I didn't know for the life of me whether I had just walked up or whether I was supposed to walk down."

Said the third woman, "I'm thankful I don't have that problem. Knock on wood." At which time she gave a few knocks on the wooden table nearby. "Excuse me, ladies," she said, "I believe I hear someone at the door."

YOUR TURN: What new things will you try?

2. *Flood your senses with experiences that cheer.* Can you be transported to the symphony via an audio or video tape? Music is a grand accompaniment to life. It can exhilarate and lift the spirit. Remember, the music David played on his harp soothed the troubled spirit of King Saul. Can you feel the warmth of the sun on your body, the cool gentle wind brushing your face? God surrounds us with His manifold gifts. Having eyes, let us look and see; having ears, let us hear and

listen; having a nose, let us sniff and smell; having hands, let us touch and feel; having a tongue, let us eat and taste. Heighten your awareness of the delights which come through your God-given senses.

Young children grow best in a positive environment. You can walk into a house where a family resides and immediately give a weather report. The climate is either warm and sunny or cloudy and stormy.

Adults thrive best in a warm, sunny climate whether at home or in the workplace. The climate is warm and sunny if people feel safe and secure—if they feel they belong and have some sense of ownership and control over their lives.

Even elderly adults in nursing homes live longer when they still have some control over their lives. Getting to make selections from a menu for what they will eat each meal helps them feel in control of some part of their lives.

3. *Learn how to have fun—the kind that makes the heart merry.* Jack Taylor of Ministries Today has suggested an 11th commandment. "Thou shalt have fun!" He called attention to several Scriptures related to the subject: "The whale you made to play in the sea" (Ps. 104:26, TLB). The *New International Version* says "to frolic." "I was glad when they said to me, 'Let us go to the house of the Lord [church]' " (Ps. 122:1). "Rejoice in the Lord always; again I will say, Rejoice!" (Phil. 4:4)

Taylor suggests two possible reasons why many people have not become Christians. They either have never known a Christian, or they have known a Christian. Who should be more joyful, more fun-loving, more happy than one who has the best of both worlds?

YOUR TURN: Make a schedule of "fun things" you will do this week.

If you want a real challenge, read the book *The Humor of Christ* by Elton Trueblood.

4. *Learn how to give.* Give not until it hurts, but until there is joy in giving. Some people give a lot of themselves and their money and begrudge every bit. They feel used and abused. The attitude of the heart makes the difference. Paul said it this way, "Let each one do just as he has purposed in his heart; not grudgingly or under compulsion; for God loves a cheerful giver" (2 Cor. 9:7).

The thrilling truth about giving generously, both of yourself and your money, is: God will grant you the desires of your heart.

Paul assures us of this in the following verse: "God is able to make all grace abound to you, that always having all sufficiency in everything, you may have an abundance for every good deed; as it is written, 'He scattered abroad, He gave to the poor, His righteousness abides forever' " (2 Cor. 9:8-9). Thank God for the gift of life which He has given you and give yourself as a gift back to Him.

YOUR TURN: What have you given this week—of yourself (your time, interest, attention)? Of your means (money or things)? How did you feel about giving what you gave? In what ways would you like to give more of yourself or what you have?

IN EVERYTHING GIVE THANKS

The apostle Paul wrote his letter of joy to the Philippians when he was imprisoned in Rome. Can you give thanks for every experience of your life?

My husband and I went to the funeral home to visit a friend whose husband had just died. This courageous widow greeted us giving thanks for the doctors who had done everything they could and for friends who had "been there" when she needed them.

For the first time I met our friend's daughter. I mentioned several names of people I knew who were members of her church. The former pastor of her church had been a long-time pastor and distinguished preacher. She shared with me a story which she said her present pastor enjoys telling on himself. This is how I remember it.

Visiting the former pastor during his last illness along with two other ministers, her pastor said he wished there were some way the distinguished preacher's brain could be transferred to his head. Maintaining his wit to the very end, the older pastor's quick response was, "That would be like putting a baby grand piano in a closet."

This story and the laughter that followed reminded the widow of a funny story which she told about the older pastor's trip in a snowstorm when he was leading a revival in the area. The laughter relieved for a moment the grief over her loss, and she returned to thoughts of thanksgiving for the many years she had enjoyed with her husband. She concluded by saying, "We didn't have much, but we had love."

The few days of sorrow and sadness do not cancel the many days of joy and gladness. Sadness and sorrow are brief. Joy is forever.

YOUR TURN: What did you give thanks for this week? What was the most difficult experience of your week? How is God working it for your good?

CREATE A POSITIVE IMAGE

Think of yourself as happy. Feel happy and act happy. When you begin thinking and feeling happy, you will act happy. Let your smiling face express enthusiasm, friendliness, and good will; and, in turn, you will receive the same. Have you noticed when watching someone smile or hearing someone laugh on TV that you find yourself smiling or laughing, too?

Greet others cheerfully. A cheery greeting initiates the "domino effect." You touch a life for good and the next one passes the loving on.

Remember that what you are now is what you are becoming.

LIVE WITH EXPECTANCY

When you are open to God's will and the prayer of your heart is: "I am yours, Lord; do with me as you will," you will experience God's miracle in each day.

God will go before you in all things. When you feel that the enemy is at your back and the sea lies ahead, you can be assured that God is going to part the waters and let you walk across on dry ground.

When you give your best efforts and leave the outcome to God, expect the most rewarding and affirming experiences to come your way. Be spontaneous in what you do, an instrument through which God can work, knowing that God and you are enough for all of your experiences.

A tape inside me continually plays this message: "God is giving you the desires of your heart. Stand back and watch the waters part."

Await with expectancy how God will work through you this day.

12

FACE PROBLEMS AS OPPORTUNITIES

"Trust in the Lord with all your heart, And do not lean on your own understanding. In all your ways acknowledge Him, And He will make your paths straight" (Prov. 3:5-6).

Last year I spent my first Christmas morning alone. This was by design. Planning to have our family together on the day after Christmas, my husband drove from Nashville to Dallas, Texas, to pick up his sister and on to Shreveport, Louisiana, to pick up LeAnn, our daughter, and our precious grandchildren, McIntyre and Rachel. Our son-in-law, a surgery resident, had to remain on duty. Mark would arrive on Christmas night. Don, our oldest, and his Heather, our other precious grandchild, and Lucia would arrive on the evening of the 26th.

Three years ago when my husband, Fred, was in depression, the children came home to celebrate an early Christmas. On a snowy Christmas Eve, they returned to their homes. A deep loneliness overwhelmed me. Bracing myself against another possibility of such a desperate feeling, I busied myself in the kitchen preparing food for the four-day visit of our loved ones. The milk was scalding for the corn pudding, the skillet was heating for the corn bread. Making every second count I measured and poured a cup of sugar into a saucepan over a burner. This was the first step in preparing fresh cranberry sauce.

When I smelled something burning, I discovered that I had turned on the burner under the saucepan instead of the one under the skillet. What a wonderful burnt sugar aroma filled the room!

Heretofore, I would have said to myself, "How stupid!" I chose, however, to say, "So I have a problem. How can I solve it? Let's see. I smell caramel. Maybe this is the beginning of a wonderful caramel pudding." And sure enough in my trusted microwave cookbook was the recipe I needed. The first step was directions for browning sugar.

What started out to be fresh cranberry sauce became a tasty caramel dessert. When life gives you burnt sugar, turn it into caramel.

During an out-of-town conference, I used my station wagon to transport writers and resources to and from the meeting place to our hotel. I discovered that the rear door window would not raise.

Before leaving the city, I determined that I would solve the problem and got greasy in my attempt. I stopped to wash my hands before heading home. Somewhat jittery from working as a mechanic, I returned to the car, and as I was backing out, scraped the fender of a new car parked alongside.

With license number in hand, I went back inside and had the owner paged. Responding to the page was a man whom I had seen before— none other than the president of the the organization sponsoring the conference. "Oh, Dr.," I responded, "I have heard you speak many times. I have always wanted to meet you, but this was not what I had in mind."

Gracious and gentle in his response to my report of the accident, we walked to the car to assess the damage.

After expressing my regret and assuring him that I would care for the damage, he said, "This is my wife's car and I will chat with her and then get back with you."

Shortly thereafter I received a redemptive letter from the president which first expressed gratitude to me for the work I was doing and then went on to say, "I talked with my wife, and we both agreed now that the car has been scratched a little, we will be able to enjoy it more."

"When life gives you lemons, turn it into lemonade." "Bloom where you are planted." "Make hay while the sun shines." You perhaps can add to this list of sayings which invite you to turn problems into opportunities or to make the most of a situation.

Life presents us with constant opportunities as we inevitably face one problem after another. If you live long enough, you will be touched by the typical crises common to man. Among these are death, disease, mental illness, handicaps, hardships, broken relationships, frustration, excessive fear, separation and divorce, natural disaster, as well as moral, social, and financial failures. You can choose to moan and groan and say, "Woe is me" or "Poor me," or you can choose to work on solutions.

In the book *The Road Less Traveled* M. Scott Peck introduces a chapter with "Life is difficult." When you recognize and accept this as one of the great truths, you can face difficulties as a challenge. Confronting and solving problems can be both painful and joyful. Do you find yourself avoiding problems because of anticipated emotional suffering? Mental and spiritual health is a matter of handling problems—of experiencing the pain, unpleasantness, and discomfort to achieve the healing and joy which follow.

Self-discipline means doing the difficult tasks first. Only then you fully appreciate the value of re-creation. Postponing pleasure and play until work is completed is a sign of self-discipline. We learn this best as children. Relaxation can be fully appreciated when contrasted with the demands of work. Too much time spent in leisure activities becomes boring and unsatisfying. Work and play are distinguished by the effect on the mind and spirit. One person's work is another person's play. One person's play is another person's work. Life needs balance and variety.

A man full of bitterness over an unwanted divorce complains because he expects the Christian life to be joyful, and he certainly does not feel any joy.

When the Bible speaks of the suffering of those who follow Christ, the note of joy is immediately sounded. "Dear friends, do not be surprised at the painful trial you are suffering, as though something strange were happening to you. But rejoice that you participate in the sufferings of Christ, so that you may be overjoyed when his glory is revealed" (1 Pet. 4:12-13, NIV).

A PROBLEM IS A RUNG ON THE LADDER OF JOY

The widow of a minister, who felt worth only as the wife of an important person, tried to live her life through her husband's reputation. When she completed compiling his sermons for publication, she had no more reason for living. Feeling worthless, she sought seclusion in the safety of her house and gave up on life. Another widow left with five children went to work to support her family. Feeling blessed to have children, she taught them how to work and play. Each of necessity had household duties. Children need to learn how to do their own work to become responsible and independent persons. Her face lights up now when she tells me, "Can you believe that I took these five children on camping trips and vacations all by myself?" "You know," she said, "I never even thought of life being difficult. I knew what I had to do, and I did it one day at a time." Even now with the children grown and gone, she is an active retiree who is perhaps the most avid reader I know—keeping up with the latest books, as well as rediscovering the old books on living the Christian life with joy. Her word is *joy*. Noticeable throughout her house on pictures, towels, and bookmarks is the word *joy* which so describes her radiant ministry to others whom she visits or entertains and blesses in her home.

All people have problems. We experience them at different times and with different intensities. Attitude makes the difference.

In an early pastorate a member of the church became not only our family doctor but a close personal friend. During the war, this young doctor was severely wounded with shrapnel in both legs and refused the doctors' recommendation to amputate one of the legs. Throughout his life, he had a chronic sore on this leg, but only his closest friends knew. Being the only doctor in this town, he was on call night and day. His life was devoted to "the ministry of suffering." Generous with his time, his abilities, and resources, the doctor inoculated children for polio when he knew the parents could not pay. When questioned, "Why do you do this?" he said, "We are all in the bundle of life together. What helps one helps another. What hurts one hurts another."

A few years ago this doctor was diagnosed with terminal cancer and was called on to endure excruciating pain. When we would call to ask about him, he would answer briefly and honestly, then he would quickly inquire, "But I want to know about you, Fred." The doctor suffered the agony of pain which he had given his life to alleviate. When he could no longer practice medicine to relieve pain, he practiced the medicine of comfort and hope. His life was full. His life was his work—his calling. He like Paul, a fellow sufferer, could say: "I have fought the good fight, I have finished the course, I have kept the faith; in the future there is laid up for me the crown of righteousness, which the Lord, the righteous Judge, will award me on that day; and not only me, but also to all who have loved His appearing" (2 Tim. 4:7-8).

In the mall where Fred and I walk each day is a small, fenced-in area which serves as the security booth. For days as I walked past, I smiled at a handsome, young man in his late thirties in the booth who always appeared happy and jovial. One day I approached a man coming toward me in a wheelchair. This was the man whose face I had seen in the security booth. His well-proportioned body stopped just where his legs would have been. Once I offered to push his wheelchair up a ramp. He courteously declared, "Thank you, but I need the exercise."

Chatting with him often, watching him laugh and talk with people, and occasionally seeing him hold the hand of a lovely woman, I think of him as one who accepts his condition and joyfully faces life. With no legs to stand on, he stands tall.

PAIN PAVES THE WAY TO MINISTRY

When I was teaching at Eastern Kentucky University, Art Linkletter gave an inspiring lecture to students warning them against the devastating effects of drug abuse. Although that was years ago, I recall what he said about how alcohol and other drugs have different effects on different people. Some people are more vulnerable to addiction than others. He shared the tragic incident of his teenage daughter's untimely death by suicide related to drugs. He also experienced the sudden death of a son in his thirties in an automobile accident.

In the October 1988 issue of *Guideposts*, I read the touching story of a grandfather whose granddaughter Jenny had a rare lymphatic condition. Her right leg measured two feet around. The grandfather, an industrial engineer in the oil industry, applied his knowledge of fluid dynamics to what he learned from a study of the lymphatic system. He learned that the pressure in the lower leg is greater than that in the knee, and the pressure in the knee is greater than that in the thigh. Through an agonizingly slow process, he worked around the clock to develop a pump which would inflate a boot and a sleeve and exert different pressure in three areas.

A grandfather's love for a granddaughter resulted in an invention which has already helped thousands of people. Grandfather acknowledged that he did not invent the treatment alone. It came through faith in God and a lot of love. In a letter to Jenny, he reminded her of the Bible verse, "Love never gives up" (1 Cor. 13:7, GNB) and continued, "I did it because I love you Jenny. And God did it because He loves us all."

A young medical doctor chose a specialty in plastic surgery. His lovely wife, a burn victim as a child, received numerous surgeries to repair the burned area. His desire is to restore those whose burns have left them disfigured and debilitated to the best possible appearance and productivity.

Three months before her husband died with cancer, Eliza Bell Williams sat in the hospital room while her husband was undergoing another surgery. Her daughter found her sitting in a chair with her Bible writing a poem. Mrs. Williams had just read in the newspaper an article about a child with Rocky Mountain spotted fever. Having almost died from the same disease, her heart went out to the family. To comfort, witness, and minister to this family, she wrote a poem for the family and sent it to them through the mail.

Her daughter asked, "How can a person whose husband is dying think of someone else?"

DISAPPOINTMENT BECAME BLESSINGS

In the summer of 1969, Major Paul Guy Durbin, a chaplain in the United States Army, was assigned to a unit at Fort Hood, Texas. For his year and a half as an administrative chaplain, he received the merit service medal. Then he was transferred to another brigade to serve as assistant chaplain. Someone who rated his services for personnel put a derogatory remark on his Officers Efficiency Report (OER). Six months later while in training at Walter Reed Army Hospital, Major Durbin learned about the derogatory remark in his OER. He sent a disclaimer and requested that the unjust statement be removed. He was informed that the statement would remain, but the disclaimer would be part of the report.

In 1975 while serving in Bangkok, Thailand, Durbin received word that he had been passed over for promotion to lieutenant colonel—the derogatory remark was the culprit. According to policy if he were passed over again in 1976, he would have to leave the army.

Durbin's clinical training at Walter Reed Hospital prepared him emotionally for what otherwise would have been a grave disappointment. Prior to his clinical training, Major Durbin confessed that he had an inferiority complex which he described as a feeling of "low self-worth masked over with an outgoing personality." He had what he called a conversion experience. His motivation for ministry changed from fear to love. He developed a feeling of self-worth and dignity within himself which was not dependent upon verification from others although, admittedly, that helped and still does.

Major Durbin shared his plight with the bishop of the Louisiana Conference. In June of 1976, while attending the annual conference, Major Durbin was asked if he were interested in an opening at Pendleton Memorial Hospital in New Orleans beginning September 1. His clinical training at Walter Reed had prepared him for the work of hospital chaplain. Then Major Durbin received word that the military had declared that two boards had been illegally convened, and all the officers passed over in 1975 and 1976 could stay on active duty until January, at which time their records would be reviewed again. Now he had a choice. Durbin chose to accept the position at Pendleton. In December of 1976, the army promotion board promoted Major Durbin to lieutenant colonel. He was to return to duty with his promotion date retroactive to 1975. He chose to remain at Pendleton Hospital.

While continuing his work at Pendleton Hospital, Major Durbin also became the chaplain of the Louisiana National Guard and was promoted to lieutenant colonel, and after attending staff school, he was promoted to full colonel in 1984.

In February 1986, Colonel Durbin was informed that he was being considered for a new position as Army National Guard special assistant to the Army Chief of Chaplains which carried the rank of brigadier general. In June Durbin was selected, but he could not wear the rank until federal recognition by Congress. He is now the first brigadier general chaplain in the Army National Guard.

In telling me his story, the chaplain recalled the story of Joseph. Joseph's brothers sold him into slavery and told their father that Joseph had been killed. Years passed, and a famine prompted Joseph's brothers to travel to Egypt to get grain. Unknowing to the brothers, Joseph was in charge of Egypt's grain. The chaplain found solace in these words: "But Joseph said to them, 'Do not be afraid, for am I in God's place? And as for you, you meant evil against me, but God meant it for good in order to bring about this present result, to preserve many people alive'" (Gen. 50:19-20).

To face problems as opportunities:

1. Accept the reality that life is difficult—a continuous series of problems.

2. Forgive those who cause you pain and problems. Send them your love.

3. Let your problems or pain pave the way to a ministry of comfort to the suffering. People will talk to you about their similar pain. You have the marvelous opportunity of giving love, compassion, and comfort.

4. Be assured that God in His own time can work for your good that which is painful and that which was intended for evil.

People with problems await the love and comfort of those who have traveled the same road. In all your ways acknowledge our loving God. And He will continue to guide you in extraordinary ways beyond your fondest imagination on the never-ending earthly journey of getting good at being you.

YOUR TURN: What is your most pressing problem? What options do you have for facing the problem? What opportunity for good awaits you? What will you choose to do? What can you expect from God?

Celebrate. Celebrate life. Celebrate your life.

God loves you. God wants the best for you and so do I.